# Friends of the Bridegroom

Bonnie Rowan

Copyright © 2015 Bonnie Rowan

*Friends of the Bridegroom*

Printed in the USA
ISBN (Print Edition): 978-0-9961772-0-7
ISBN (Kindle): 978-0-9961772-1-4
ISBN (eBook): 978-0-9961772-2-1

Library of Congress Control Number: 2015903793

All Rights Reserved. This book is protected by the copyright laws of the United States of America. This book may not be copied or reprinted for commercial gain or profit. The use of short quotations is permitted. Permission will be granted upon request. The author guarantees all contents are original and do not infringe upon the legal rights of any other person or work.

Prepared for Publication By

PALM TREE PUBLICATIONS

Palm Tree Publications is a Division of Palm Tree Productions
www.palmtreeproductions.com
PO BOX 122 | KELLER, TX | 76244

Unless otherwise noted, Scripture references are from the New King James Version (NKJV) of the Bible. Copyright © 1982 by Thomas Nelson, Inc. Used by permission. All rights reserved.

To Contact the Author:

**www.stmtc.net**

Shepherd's Tent Ministries Training Center

*"The voice of one crying in the wilderness,*

*'Prepare the way of the Lord;*

*make His paths straight.'"*

Matt. 3:3 NKJV

"Come ye out from the wilderness," says the Lord. "Rise up from where you lie, for the time is short and My time for the harvest is near unto you. Behold, I stand at the door and knock. Come quickly, My friends, and open to Me. The wind is blowing and My sound is roaring. Why is it that you cannot hear?"

"Many believe My wind to be warfare from satan and fight against it, but you must learn the difference between the two. I am blowing things off My friends that are distracting them from the posts where I have positioned them. Many gates are about to open that have been closed and locked into the next dimension."

"I have set up towers North, East, South, and West and have placed My watchmen upon them. Listen for the sound of My trumpet, for I will be calling My people to bow before Me. I am casting off the spirit of pride from many so that their true identities will show forth. I will lead many out of darkness and into the light so they will no longer stumble and keep falling down. I desire not to stand in the shadows of your life any longer; I must have first place, for I love you with an unquenchable love."

"For behold, the light has come and the glory of the Lord is risen upon you. Rise up from your bed of comfort and come to the door that I am putting before you, for it is midnight and I am calling My Bride to come. For the mouth of the Lord has spoken it!"

# Dedication

I give all glory to God who has called me to be a friend of the Bridegroom. This book is dedicated to my husband and best friend, Ernie, whom God has put alongside me to partner in the work of the Kingdom. I also dedicate it to my four children who have taught me to love unconditionally throughout the years. I thank God for giving me these precious gifts.

# Acknowledgements

I want to honor those who have walked beside me, influenced me, and encouraged me.

- My older sister Dottie has stood with me through thick and thin. She cared for me as a child and continues to walk with me today.

- Deanna Wiles, my faithful friend and elder armor bearer has walked with me in ministry since I began. These two women are truly friends of the Bridegroom.

- I'm so thankful for the faithful congregation of Shepherd's Tent Ministries, who support me and are willing to follow the visions of their leaders.

- I also honor my pastors who are now in the cloud of witnesses, Brother Wade Taylor and Pastor Clara Wilkins. Brother Taylor has left a legacy of intimacy and desire for the presence of God, and for the sons of God to be raised up in the last days. Pastor Clara has left her mantle to her sons and daughters to carry on a passion for Israel in celebrating the feasts. I endeavor to carry on their anointings and legacies.

- Finally, I would like to acknowledge my apostles, Drs. John and Rebecca Polis, and thank them for their faithfulness in releasing the apostolic anointing to their sons and daughters.

# Praise for Friends of the Bridegroom

The message of this book is one every leader in the Body of Christ needs to have imparted to them. Bonnie Rowan has issued a practical prophetic challenge to believers to rise to maturity for the end-time harvest. I am confident the Lord has brought about this book for a "time such as this." I highly recommend it!

—MARYALICE ISLEIB
*Director, MaryAlice Ministries, Christian Outreach International*


Friends of the Bridegroom is a clarion call for the Church to rise up and be who She was originally meant to be. With sound scriptural backing, this book beckons the friends of the Bridegroom to make His Bride glorious and ready for His coming. As you read this book, you will discover insights that will encourage you to truly become a "friend of the Bridegroom."

I recommend this book to anyone desiring to understand what it is to be a friend of our Bridegroom, Jesus Christ, and who wants a deeper walk with Him. As we draw close to Him, He draws close to us and leads us into the bridal chamber of His Presence.

—APOSTLE LES BOWLING
*Eagle Rock Church, Eagle Rock Covenant Network*

Bonnie Rowan has done a masterful job of presenting a powerful concept concerning our relationship to Jesus and His church in her new book, *Friends of the Bridegroom*.

I found the book both instructive and inspiring. It had the effect of holding my interest, while at the same time, stirring my heart. I believe the Church has largely lost the thread of the love relationship of the bride and the Bridegroom. Rarely do we hear teaching on this subject.

In pictures that cannot be forgotten, Bonnie calls us to remember our commitment to our First Love. Using various appropriate scriptures in both Old and New Testaments, she convincingly explains the great privilege and responsibility of being friends of the Bridegroom.

I strongly recommend this book. Leaders will be greatly encouraged and enlightened through the understanding presented. It is also a book for everybody, in the sense that it has the power to elevate our opinion of the extreme importance of a truly spiritual relationship between Christ and His bride. The book gives clear direction to those who wait to hear His voice and serve Him as one who prepares the way for His return.

—Dr. Sue Curran
*Founding Pastor, Shekinah Church Ministries*
*Blountville, Tennessee*

Of my 64 years on this planet, 41 have been lived as a follower of Christ. During that time I have learned the value of having a true friend, and also how to be a friend to others. Being a friend is costly; it means that you will stay faithful no matter what pain or rejoicing it may bring to your life. A friend is someone with whom you can feel totally comfortable, enough so that you share your deepest joys and sorrows knowing that your friend will understand as though it was their own experience. A friend will always have your best interest at heart and will be committed to the success of your dreams as much as their own.

Being a "Friend of the Bridegroom," our Lord Jesus Christ, means these things and so much more. Apostle Bonnie Rowan has shared from her life of devotion to the Bride of Christ as one who truly knows what it means to be a "friend." I have known her for many years and have seen the depth of her love for God and His people. I have known of her many trials and sufferings which she has embraced as tools to bring her closer to the Bridegroom whom she loves. Her grasp of allegory and revelation brings forth many hidden gems of truth that will inspire a deeper passion for intimacy with the Lord.

As you read this book, Holy Spirit will unveil the steps to a greater love relationship with Him, through words of doctrine, reproof, correction and instruction in righteousness.

Thanks Apostle, for allowing your life to go through the winepress so that these riches could be revealed and shared with all of us.

—Dr. John Polis, Presiding Apostle
*Revival Fellowship International*

# Contents

1    **Introduction**

## Part One

7    Chapter One
      **Who is a Friend of the Bridegroom?**

15   Chapter Two
      **Paul: A Friend of the Bridegroom**

19   Chapter Three
      **The Little Sisters**

29   Chapter Four
      **Do You Qualify?**

## Part Two

37   Chapter Five
      **Qualification #1: Deny Ourselves**

41   Chapter Six
      **Qualification #2: Do Not Compromise**

45   Chapter Seven
      **Qualification #3: Get Delivered of Pride**

53   Chapter Eight
      **Qualification #4: Have a Heart for the Poor and Hear the Cry of Our Cities**

59   Chapter Nine
      **Qualification #5: Be Militant**

69   Chapter Ten
      **Qualification #6: Have a Heart for Prayer and Worship**

## Part Three

| | |
|---|---|
| 79 | Chapter Eleven |
| | **Those Who Represent the Friends of the Bridegroom** |
| 89 | Chapter Twelve |
| | **A Friend of God's Jewish Bride** |
| 93 | Chapter Thirteen |
| | **Who is this Mysterious Woman Named Mary?** |
| 107 | Conclusion |
| | **The Bride has Made Herself Ready** |

# Introduction

You are holding in your hands a book written for those in leadership. It has been birthed out of a great burden for the bride of Christ, and I believe it is a necessary word for this hour. I encourage you to open your heart to the working of the Holy Spirit as you read the following pages. Only He knows what will specifically minister to you.

> *God has called us to love the bride of Christ and to lay our lives down for her. Jesus said, "greater love has no man than this, that he lay down his life for his friends."*
>
> JOHN 15:13 NKJV

Who is the bride of Christ? Sometimes it's people who don't look like we want them to look; they don't always act the way we want them to act. Sometimes they hurt us, they offend us, and they betray us. Can I be a friend of the Bridegroom and care for this bride, the way He would truly have us care for her? Can I lay down my life in love for her? Can I love what He loves?

If we compare the day we are living in to the day of Noah, we see that the same thing is going on now that was going on then. By his obedience to God, Noah proved his friendship when God told him to prepare an ark and tell the people that judgment was coming. Of course, the people laughed at him and didn't believe him. They were doing anything they thought to be right in their own eyes, just as many are doing today.

> *The Lord saw that the wickedness of man was great in the earth, and that every intent of the thoughts of his heart was only evil continually.*
> Gen. 6:5 NKJV

We are living in the end time where we believe for a great revival and the wine being poured out, but we must remember that satan and his demons are also praying and waiting for their revival. As the end draws nearer, the warfare is going to get greater. As in the days of Noah, the sons of God began to take daughters of men and they brought forth giants in the land. This is also happening today. When we are saved and filled with the Holy Spirit, and we turn from God and become a partaker of deliberate sin, we take on the image of the world (the daughters of men). When we play in the world, we bring forth after our own kind. If our ministries are mixed with the world, we will birth a generation of people who cannot discern good from evil.

Noah didn't wait until it started to rain to build the ark; he obeyed God and got started right away. Those of us who are in fivefold ministry must tell people the truth about what is happening today. Today is the day of salvation. The friends of the Bridegroom, like Noah, are called to build an ark of safety. The ark that we are called to build may not be like the one Noah built, but just as God gave instructions on how to build the ark, He has also told us how to build His Church.

The House of God must be built upon His Word. Although Noah knew he would be mocked and ridiculed, he was still not willing to compromise the Word of the Lord. Some today are saying the Old Testament stories no longer apply to us, but this story of Noah made its way into the New Testament, so I think we need to listen and respond to it. Those who did not respond to Noah's cry were left behind to die in the judgment of God. Only the household of Noah made it through the flood. It's time to believe and prepare ourselves now. The Bible is true and judgment is coming to the earth, whether we believe it or not.

> *Is there a heaven and hell? Could a God of love allow us to go into a burning hell forever? Is it true that I can be saved and turn from God and still go to heaven? I, for one, believe in a burning hell and I do believe there will be those on the Day of Judgment who will say, "'Lord, Lord, have we not prophesied in Your name, cast out demons in Your name, and done many wonders in Your name?' And then [Jesus] will declare to them, 'I never knew you; depart from Me, you who practice lawlessness.'"*
> MATTHEW 7:22-23 NKJV

Let the friends of the Bridegroom rise up and begin to intercede for a revival to be poured out upon our dry and weary land! Let the spirit of John the Baptist be heard in our land:

> *The voice of one crying in the wilderness: Prepare the way of the Lord; Make straight in the desert a highway for our God. Every valley shall be exalted And every mountain and hill brought low; The crooked places shall be made straight and the rough places*

> *smooth; The glory of the Lord shall be revealed, and all flesh shall see it together; For the mouth of the Lord has spoken.*
>
> ISAIAH 40:3-5; MATT. 3:3 NKJV

The Greek word "prodromos" means "forerunner; scout; guide; one sent before a king to prepare the way." It could also mean "first fruits." We are to be the forerunners for Jesus' return in this end time just as John the Baptist prepared the way for His coming. We must make the paths straight for Jesus to come. Our voice must be heard in the land. We can't just lead people to salvation and not take them any farther. John said to bring forth fruits worthy of repentance (see Matt. 3:8). It is the responsibility of the friends of the Bridegroom to make sure the people are being told the truth and are walking in it. We are to make disciples, not just followers. When the prodigal came home, he was not allowed to bring the pigs into his father's house. He left the pigs in the pig pen and came home.

I know you are probably thinking that when sinners get saved, they don't know how to walk in Christ. When we were sinners we were dead, but as soon as we are saved, our spirit man comes alive in us and we know the truth. We have to grow from babies into maturity, but we should not have a desire to continue in sin if we are truly born again. I did not know the Word of God when I got saved, but I can tell you that I didn't want to do the things that I did before. I fell in love with God and my image was changed, and is being changed every day, from glory to glory.

> *For it is the God who commanded light to shine out of darkness, who has shone in our hearts to give the light of the knowledge of the glory of God in the face of Jesus Christ.*
>
> 2 COR. 4:6 NKJV

# Part One

Chapter One

# Who is the Friend of the Bridegroom?

*"He who has the bride is the Bridegroom; but the friend of the bridegroom, who stands and hears him, rejoices greatly because of the bridegroom's voice. Therefore this joy of mine is fulfilled."*

JOHN 3:29 NKJV

I think we have all wondered at some time or another just whom God is calling the friends of the Bridegroom. Of course we know that John the Baptist was considered to be a friend of the Bridegroom. But who are the friends of today? We are now living in what I believe to be our end time. If that is the case, the Bridegroom (Jesus) is coming to get His bride very soon. Oh my! Will she be ready? I ask that question with much concern for the bride. My heart is sometimes very heavy and saddened for her.

Who are the friends of the Bridegroom? They are those in fivefold ministry whom God has called to equip the saints and bring His bride into maturity so that she might be presented to Him without spot, blemish, or wrinkle. They are also the ones (who may not be in fivefold ministry) who are so in love with Jesus that they are willing to lay down their lives for the bride, no matter the cost.

The friends of the Bridegroom must be groomed by the hand of the Master, the Father of the Bridegroom. Those who have been called to help the Father prepare for the heavenly wedding must go through much training and fire. After all, the friend of the Bridegroom must be proven trustworthy. How else could he be allowed in the dressing room of such a great man of royalty? This great event has been in preparation for many years. And just as John the Baptist was chosen long before he was ever conceived, we are too.

> *A friend of the Bridegroom must be proven trustworthy.*

The Father knew from the very beginning of time exactly what year, day, and time this wedding would take place. He will not be surprised, but I believe many of His people will. Some who are called to help prepare His bride have not passed the test, and have not been found trustworthy to be in the chambers with Him. As I have studied and prayed about the friends of the Bridegroom, God has given me some insight as to who these friends are and what the qualifications are to be counted such a friend. There are people throughout the pages of the Bible who show signs that they are friends of the Bridegroom. There are also signs that show us who His friends are today. Maybe we have not been ready until now to ask God, "Where are the friends of the Bridegroom?"

> *And He said to them, "Fill the water pots with water." And they filled them up to the brim. And He said to them, "Draw some out now, and take it to the master of the feast." And they took it.*
>
> JOHN 2:7-8 NKJV

The marriage feast is just about to start, the water has been turned to wine, and only the servants (the friends) know where it came from. How did they know? They knew because they heard and were obedient to what Jesus told them to do. They weren't distracted by the party and the great men who were there. They weren't looking for attention from one of the influential guests, nor did they take the credit for the great wine and try to sell it.

John 3:29 tells us that they rejoiced greatly because they heard the Bridegroom's voice: *"He who has the bride is the bridegroom; but the friend of the bridegroom, who stands and hears him, rejoices greatly because of the bridegroom's voice, therefore this joy of mine is fulfilled"* (NKJV).

We see in the Scripture that the friends of the bridegroom were standing and they were hearing. This means they were attentive to the bridegroom's needs and what he desired. Among believers today, it doesn't seem to be as much about the Bridegroom as it is about the wants and desires of His servants, those who should be helping to make everything safe and ready for the Bridegroom to take His bride. John the Baptist said, "He must increase, but I must decrease" (John 3:30 NKJV). In the coming pages, we will be talking a lot about John because he is the perfect pattern of what God expects out of His friends.

> *And He Himself gave some to be apostles, some prophets, some evangelists, and some pastors and teachers, for the equipping of the saints for the work of ministry, for the edifying of the body of Christ, till we all come*

> to the unity of the faith and of the knowledge of the Son of God, to a perfect man, to the measure of the stature of the fullness of Christ.
>
> EPHESIANS 4:11-13 NKJV

In the New Testament Church, Jesus Himself set in order the prophets and apostles. They were to birth and train other apostles, prophets, evangelists, pastors and teachers, patterned after themselves and carved out of Jesus, the Cornerstone. When Jesus told Peter, *"upon this rock I will build My church and the gates of hell shall not prevail against it"* (Matt. 16:18 NKJV), He was speaking of the revelation of Himself that Peter had received. But as the years have passed, the ones whom Jesus has trusted to care for and to watch over His bride until His return, have been tossed out of the church and replaced with man-made programs.

## Prepare for the Bridegroom's Return

It's time for the Bridegroom to return, and we have a job to do. It is time for the fivefold ministers to wake up, get up, and get cleaned up. It's not about who can acquire the biggest platform or the most prestige. It's about loving the Body of Christ enough to lay our lives down for her. My concern is not whether I can sin and still make it to heaven; it's that I would have an ear to hear what the Bridegroom is saying to the Church and be obedient to Him.

Would you want someone who is blind leading your bride, staggering around trying to take her to the marriage feast? I don't think so! The Word says *"If the blind lead the blind they will both fall into the ditch"* (Matthew 15:14 NKJV). From the foundation of the earth, the friends of the Bridegroom have been called to care for the bride, and they must keep themselves clean and untouched by the world.

Can you imagine what it must be like to get engaged to the woman of your dreams, only to find that while you'd gone away, she'd been left unattended and vulnerable for other men to attack, rape, and steal the dowry that she was preparing for you? As I have been studying and praying for His bride, this is the picture I have seen.

God Himself has chosen friends of the Bridegroom and placed them strategically in His Kingdom on earth. He has called friends of the bride and the Bridegroom to care for His bride until He returns to take her to the home He has prepared. There are instructions and requirements all through the Word of God as to how He would have us to care for His bride. The first requirement is that we have clean hands so as not to cause more spots and blemishes on her than what she already has.

There has not been much teaching on the friends whom God has called to take care of things here on the earth while He is getting things ready for His return. I believe it's the midnight hour and if there has ever been a time that we've needed to stay awake and watch, it is now. The friends on earth today are rising up as a corporate John the Baptist, a voice crying in the wilderness, *"prepare ye the way of the Lord!"* (Isaiah 40:3 KJV).

I have always had a great love for the bride of Christ and what she means to God. But over the past few years, God has been troubling my heart about the ones He has called to lay down their lives for the bride. The Bible says that in the last days deceiving spirits would come and many would fall away from the faith. Many of those called to equip the bride are being taken out by deceiving demonic spirits. Men of God whom I have respected greatly have turned their backs on the bride of Christ. I believe God's heart is very grieved. This is evident in Paul's writings. As he laid his life down for the bride, Paul pleaded with the leaders to keep themselves clean.

> *Command those who are rich in this present age not to be haughty, nor to trust in uncertain riches but in the living God, who gives us richly all things to enjoy.*
> 1 Timothy 6:17 NKJV

It is God's heart that we have prosperity and be happy with it, but the love of money and fame is turning God's leaders away from the faith and filling their hearts with pride. God wants us to prosper so that we might do the work of the Kingdom here on earth. Our hearts must be for the bride of Christ because that is where God's heart is. There are people today who are saying they don't like the Church or the commandments upon which it is built. It really grieves my heart to think that a generation is being deceived into thinking the Church is too old-fashioned for the modern world. But I tell you, it is the real Church (the ecclesia) who will still be standing when the world and all its glory and perversion has passed away.

## Questions for Reflection

1. "The friends of the bridegroom were standing and they were hearing." In what ways are you attentive to the Bridegroom (Jesus)?

   _____

   _____

2. "God wants us to prosper so that we might do the work of the Kingdom here on earth. Our hearts must be for the bride of Christ because that is where God's heart is." What is your heart seeking after?

   _____

   _____

3. "There are people today who are saying they don't like the Church or the commandments upon which it is built." How do you feel about the Body of Christ?

   _____

   _____

## Chapter Two

# Paul: A Friend of the Bridegroom

*For I am jealous for you with godly jealousy. For I have betrothed you to one husband, that I may present you as a chaste virgin to Christ.*

2 CORINTHIANS 11:2 NKJV

Paul was definitely a friend of the Bridegroom, and we can hear his heart for the bride in his writing. In his jealousy, Paul pleaded with the Church not to go after deceiving spirits of the world because they would defile her. A man of great tribulation, Paul was so rich in the love of Jesus. He had one purpose for being alive after he met Jesus, and that was to die daily and to preach the Gospel of Christ. He loved the Church and was willing to give his life for her.

When we have been marked by God to be one of the friends of the Bridegroom, we will experience much training and testing throughout our lives, not only when we give our hearts to God. God begins to groom us from the very beginning, just as He did Moses and all His other great leaders throughout the Bible. I have learned as I have walked with God for over forty years that my life is not my own; it has been bought with a great price. I have learned not to be angry and bitter, or to question God about why I have gone through the things that I have gone through. My life has not been easy, but it has been very profitable for the Kingdom of God. I realize as I am starting into my mature years, that all of it has been for my training, to make me into a friend of the Bridegroom, and how awesome that is!

> *We are living in a day when everyone wants everything to be so easy ...*

We are living in a day when everyone wants everything to be so easy that we never get our spiritual muscles built up to get us through difficult times. People are escaping with drugs and alcohol. We are even escaping with the doctrine of the rapture. I'm not saying that it is wrong to believe in this if it is the doctrine of your church. I am saying that we can't use it as an escape, or it is no better than a drug. For some, the message of prosperity can also be a hiding place. Prosperity is wonderful and I believe in it, but it has no power to heal me or save me.

God is calling out friends of the Bridegroom in this season to prepare for His appearing. When He left His bride here to get prepared for the great wedding, He said He would return at a time when we would not be expecting Him. He told us we would know by the signs that He would send us. I think we have been seeing all the signs and wonders. Those who have accepted the call to work alongside Him in the end times will suffer persecution and some major storms in their lives. Don't complain, because you have signed up for this at one time or another, or God wouldn't have you led you here! Remember, when we say yes to God in one season, we have to make sure we are able to say yes in the next. Friends of the Bridegroom will endure hardship, but oh, the glory that we will experience! It will be worth it all; are we ready?

> *Behold, now is the accepted time; behold, now is the day of salvation. We give no offense in anything, that our ministry may not be blamed. But in all things we commend ourselves as ministers of God: in much patience, in tribulations, in needs, in distresses. in stripes, in imprisonments, in tumults, in labors, in sleeplessness, in fastings; by purity, by knowledge, by longsuffering, by kindness, by the Holy Spirit, by sincere love, by the word of truth, by the power of God, by the armor of righteousness on the right hand and on the left, by honor and dishonor, by evil report and good report; as deceivers, and yet true; as unknown, and yet well known; as dying, and behold we live; as chastened, and yet not killed; as sorrowful, yet always rejoicing; as poor, yet making many rich; as having nothing, and yet possessing all things.*
>
> 2 Corinthians 6:2-10 nkjv

Wow, isn't that something? I am not trying to depress you, but if we are in ministry and God has called us, we are going to go through some things. A good father does not tell his children that everything is going to be a bed of roses out there in the world. If he did, and his children grew up believing this, they would never make it through life when hard times came. If we are called and marked to be in fivefold ministry, God will train and test us. We will all have difficult seasons, but if we press toward God, He will take us through them with victory.

As we read Paul's writings, we see how God was training him to be an apostle while he was yet persecuting the Church. He trained Paul for that season even before he was saved. We've seen what was required of Paul to be a friend. As we go farther, we will find other friends of the Bridegroom.

## Questions for Reflection

1. "I have learned not to be angry and bitter, or to question God about why I have gone through the things that I have gone through." Have your life experiences left you with any residue of bitterness or anger?

   _____

   _____

2. "We are living in a day when everyone wants everything to be so easy that we never get our spiritual muscles built up to get us through difficult times." Are your spiritual muscles built up? Are there things that you do to try to escape difficulties?

   _____

   _____

3. "Remember, when we say yes to God in one season, we have to make sure we are able to say yes in the next." What are some times when you've said yes to God?

   _____

   _____

## Chapter Three

# The Little Sisters

*We have a little sister, and she has no breasts. What shall we do for our sister in the day when she is spoken for? If she is a wall, we will build upon her a battlement of silver; and if she is a door, we will enclose her with boards of cedar.*

Song of Solomon 8:8-9 NKJV

How wonderful it is to think that God has called us for this day and to a special time and season, just as He did John the Baptist. This is the most glorious time one could ever live in. God has been planning for this day since Adam and Eve were deceived by the enemy in the Garden and gave up their destiny. Since that time, God has been adorning the bride for His Son, the one taken out of His side. Just as God called Adam to care for the garden, dress it, and develop it, He has called those who will be obedient to Him and care for His bride. You might say, "I thought everyone who is saved is part of the bride." But have you asked, "Who are the sons, who are the handmaidens, who are the servants, and who are the fivefold ministers?"

The friends of the Bridegroom are those who surrender their lives as Jesus did for His bride. They are the ones who yearn for the manifest presence (parousia) of God. They do not hide from His glory even though they know His glory comes to kill their flesh. Because of their great love for the Bridegroom, they have endured times of great testing. As they have walked through the darkness with God, they have learned to discern His smell, His sound, His touch, and His glory. They have learned that submission is freedom and not bondage. They give their lives to find their lives in Him. They continue to seek His face while their hands are empty. They do not look for a title; they allow their titles to look for them. His friends know that the title is not who they are, but rather what they have become in Him. God shares the secrets of His heart to those who have become trusted friends and companions.

To some, God entrusts a small portion of His glorious bride, knowing that they need more care than others. But there are those whom He is testing to see if they will be faithful over little, in order that He might give them more. In Song of Solomon, the Shulamite maiden is very concerned with the little sister who is immature and not yet able to feed others or discern good from evil. When she inquires as to how to care for this sister, the answer she gets is not, "walk away from her because you have been called to a much higher ministry." He tells her to lay her life down for this little one until she is strong enough to stand.

> *We have a little sister, and she has no breasts. What shall we do for our sister in the day when she is spoken for? If she is a wall, we will build upon her a battlement of silver; and if she is a door, we will enclose her with boards of cedar.*
>
> SONG OF SOLOMON 8:8-9 NKJV

The Shulamite maiden is told to enclose her with boards of cedar. This speaks of those who have been strengthened in the Lord and have gone from glory to glory, and have put their roots down deep in love and obedience to the Bridegroom. The cedar tree was used in the building of Solomon's temple. The cedar grows very high toward heaven and its roots are as long as the tree is high. If we do not have our roots deep in Jesus and we grow high in recognition, we will be filled with pride and we will fall. If we are going to be friends of the Bridegroom, we must endure the storms of life the enemy brings to try to turn us away from God. We must come through our storms with the praises of our wonderful Savior on our lips. The wind blows upon the cedar tree but it stands because of its strong roots, just as we will stand if our roots are planted deep into the Kingdom of God.

*If our roots are planted deep into the Kingdom of God, we will stand.*

The allegory also speaks of the little sister being a door. This is saying that she is swinging, not yet stable and she needs someone to enclose her with their own strength until she becomes strong enough in God's Word to stand on her own. We are to lay our lives down for those who are weak until they become strong in their faith. This little sister is part of the Bride of Christ that is being groomed for Him, she is just immature.

The friends of the Bridegroom are careful not to share much meat with the little sisters, lest these young ones become violent and turn on them, and this would grieve the heart of God. There is much training to be done before God will trust His servants with His Son's bride. I believe this is why He has prolonged His coming, to allow time for His bride to be dressed and ready for Him. All the signs point to His coming.

Many today are getting her drunk on the wine of the world, stimulating the bride with messages that only tickle her ears. But it is time to stop playing with the bride and get her ready for her Bridegroom. She must be clothed in truth and righteousness, not in peasants' garments. Friends of the Bridegroom must stand at the door and announce, *"Behold the Bridegroom is coming; go out to meet Him!"* (Matthew 25:6 NKJV).

> *Then I, John, saw the holy city, New Jerusalem, coming down out of heaven from God, prepared as a bride adorned for her husband.*
> REVELATION 21:2 NKJV

The friends of the Bridegroom are to teach the bride how to be intimate with her Beloved. The friends of Jesus praise Him to her and they never take any credit for themselves. They watch over the chambers so that no one enters to defile it or make it impure.

When Prince William and Duchess Kate were expecting their royal baby, her delivery room was sealed off and guards stood by the door to see that no one entered. Everything in it was sterilized and kept pure until it was time for the duchess to birth the baby into the royal family. When she came out, her son was presented to the whole world. This is what will happen when the bride is brought out of the wilderness. The whole world will see her as she stands with her Bridegroom, Jesus.

We are hidden and veiled by our flesh, but God is building His holy throne within us. We, as the sons of God, are being birthed out of the earth man and into the Kingdom man. Do you know that a woman's womb is a sterile and safe place for a baby to develop? When we receive salvation, we enter into a spiritual place that is pure, called "the holy place" (Jesus). There we grow and mature while awaiting His arrival.

> *Jesus answered and said to him, "Most assuredly, I say to you, unless one is born again, he cannot see the kingdom of God."*
> JOHN 3:3 NKJV

Paul also talked about birthing the second time in Galatians:

> *"My little children, for whom I labor in birth again until Christ is formed in you."*
> GALATIANS 4:19 NKLV

The subject of birthing the sons of God seems to be a mystery. When this is mentioned in the Word, it is simply talking about growing into maturity so that we can walk with Him as Adam and Eve did while in the garden. Adam was given authority over everything. He was to be fruitful and multiply and replenish the earth. Today God is calling those who will help bring His bride into maturity. There are many callings in the company of the bride and Groom but they must be birthed through the Spirit, not through man-made programs or man-induced callings. The Bible says, *"Many are called, but few are chosen"* (Matthew 22:14 NKJV). Man cannot preach unless he is called, or he will have no revelation to preach (see Romans 10:14-15).

I long for the manifest presence of God to be birthed in me. In his book *Waterspouts of Glory*, Wade Taylor describes God's preparation of His people: "We are privileged to live in the time of the "Parousia" (presence) of our Lord Jesus Christ. The "manifested presence" of the Lord will precede His personal return. A called out body of "overcomers" is being prepared to manifest His presence in the earth, which will lead to the establishing of His Millennial Kingdom."[1] Jesus will be fully revealed *"when He shall come to be glorified in His saints"* (2 Thessalonians 1:10 KJV).

I believe this book you are reading is a timely rhema word from the Lord. It is time for His friends to step up to the front lines to either be invited to serve in the marriage feast or to be disqualified. Maybe you have been going through storms for what has seemed like forever, or maybe you are still waiting for your preaching platform, knowing that

God has called you. If this describes you, you have probably been in great testing and have been being groomed for this season.

Years ago while in Bible school, I read a pamphlet written by Bill Britton entitled *The Harness of the Lord*. It was one of the best allegories I'd ever read concerning the discipline of the Lord and I would like to share it with you.

## The Harness of the Lord[2]

The vision began with a carriage on a dirt road, adorned with beautiful carvings edged with gold. It was pulled by six large horses, two in the lead, two in the middle and two in the rear. The carriage was stopped and as he looked closer, he saw the driver lying on the ground behind the last two horses' heels, working on something. He thought to himself, "He is in a dangerous place, for if one of those horses moves, he could get killed." The horses did not move because they were trained and he could trust them. The horses were not acting restless, and though they had bells on their feet, the bells were not tinkling. There were pom-poms on their harnesses over their heads, but the pom-poms were not moving. They were waiting for the voice of the master.

Next he saw two young colts in an open field, who approached the carriage and seemed to say to the horses, "come and play with us; we have many fine games." And with that, the colts kicked up their heels, flicked their tails and raced across the open field. But when they looked back, they didn't understand why the groomed horses were not following them. The young colts knew nothing of the harness and they were puzzled by it. Amongst themselves, they made fun of the other horses and called them weak. But the mature horses didn't say a word and they didn't move. They were waiting for their master's voice to tell them when to go forward.

The scene changed and a noose was being put around the colts' necks and they were being led off to the master's corral for training. There they were put in confinement as the trainer began to work on them with his whip and his bridle. The colts could not understand the reason for this terrible discipline. All they could see was the tightness of the corral and the trainer's strong hand on them. Little did they know of the responsibility that was to be theirs when they were fully submitted to the discipline of the master and would finish their training.

One of the colts rebelled under the training and said, "This is not for me. I like my freedom." So he jumped the fence and ran back to the meadows. The master let him go and then gave all his attention to the remaining colt. Even though this colt had the same opportunity to escape, he had decided to submit to the ways of the master. He was learning to respond to even the quietness of the man's voice. Had there been no training and no testing, there would have been neither submission nor rebellion from either of the colts. In the field they did not have the choice to rebel or submit, they were sinless in their innocence. But when brought to the place of testing, training, and discipline, the obedience of one and the rebellion of the other were manifested. It seemed safer not to come to the place of discipline because of the risk of being found rebellious, yet without this there could be no sharing of his glory.

> *Without the place of discipline, there can be no sharing of God's glory.*

Finally the training was over and instead of being sent back to the fields, the horse entered into a greater confinement than ever. A harness was dropped around his neck and he found that now there was not even freedom to run around the small corral, for in the harness he could only move where and when his master spoke. Unless the master spoke, he stood still.

As the scene changed, the other colt was standing on the side of the hill, and as he looked up he saw the king's carriage being pulled by six beautiful horses. Much to his amazement, his brother colt was leading the entire team. His brother had become strong and mature on the corn in the master's stable. He saw the lovely pom-poms shaking in the wind, and the glittering gold-bordered harness around his brother's neck…and envy filled his heart.

The undisciplined colt complained to himself. "Why has my brother been so honored, and I am rejected? They haven't put bells on *my* feet, or pom-poms on *my* head. The master has not given *me* the wonderful responsibility of pulling his carriage, nor put about my neck the golden harness. Why have they chosen my brother instead of me? He got this answer, "Because one submitted to the will and discipline of the master, and one rebelled, thus has one been chosen and the other set aside."

The two colts represent the obedient and disobedient people of the Lord. As the Bible says, of the two men working in the field; one will be taken and the other left (see Matthew 24:40 NKJV). The carriage and the king represent Jesus in the day of His coming, whether it be the fulfillment of our destinies or His return at the end of time. Just as the colts were put in a corral to train them and to test their obedience, God has also been training a people for years for His coming. This training could also be training for the great end-time harvest God has promised. Let's not miss it!

## Endnotes

1. Wade Taylor, *Waterspouts of Glory* (Hughesville, PA: Wade Taylor Publications, 2005),p.ix.
2. Bill Britton, *The Harness of the Lord*. Used by permission.

## Questions for Reflection

1. "They have learned that submission is freedom and not bondage." What comes to mind when you think of submission?

   _____

   _____

2. "We must come through our storms with the praises of our wonderful Savior on our lips." What do you do when storms come?

   _____

   _____

3. "But when brought to the place of testing, training, and discipline, the obedience of one (colt) and the rebellion of the other were manifested." Which of these two colts do you identify with the most?

   _____

   _____

## Chapter Four

# Do You Qualify?

*"Till we all come in the unity of the faith, and of the knowledge of the Son of God, to a perfect man, to the measure of the stature of the fullness of Christ."*

EPHESIANS 4:13 NKJV

The bride must come to full maturity before the Church Age can come to an end. Only the Father will decide when that will be. Much depends on the ones whom God has called to equip the saints. There are people within a people who have given themselves over to become the full expression of God. Only when we yield ourselves to the working of the Cross will we be able to lay our lives down for others. Only then will we be given access to the deeper things of the Kingdom. I will elaborate more on this later.

> *And as we have borne the image of the man of dust, we
> shall also bear the image of the heavenly Man.*
> 1 Corinthians 15:49 NKJV

Everyone is not willing to abide in the secret place of the Most High God because this is a place where we become transparent before Him. Here is where we find out if we are able to drink of the cup from which He drank and to be baptized with the same baptism with which He was baptized. Here He will require much more from us than just being nominal Christians. He will ask us if we are willing to eat His flesh and drink His blood. If we do not have a revelation of who He truly is, we will do just as many of the disciples did—we will walk away!

> *"He who eats My flesh and drinks My blood abides in
> Me, and I in him;" From that time many of His disciples
> went back and walked with Him no more.*
> John 6:56, 66 NKJV

If we are going to be a friend of the Bridegroom, we must know Him so well that we know how to abide in His presence. This comes from spending time with Him, coming away from all the distractions of the world. It is easy to get caught up in the things of the world, especially when they seem to be what preaching the Gospel is about today. But if we are not abiding in His presence, we will find ourselves like the multitude who only desired the bread and fish.

If you are one who truly believes in holiness and righteousness and does not compromise the Word of God, you will not be too popular. More than likely, you will be persecuted by those looking for the broad gate instead of the narrow way. God's Word does not change for a generation of new preachers who want to be rich and famous, even at the expense of their salvation. Many today are falling for the doctrine that teaches that no one goes to hell anymore. They are preaching that Jesus died for us and paid for our sins, which I believe with all my heart, but I also believe there is no salvation without repentance. Jesus Himself tells us what is required. We need only to follow Him and His teachings.

> *"Enter by the narrow gate; for wide is the gate and broad is the way that leads to destruction, and there are many who go in by it. Because narrow is the gate and difficult is the way which leads to life, and there are few who find it."*
> MATTHEW 7:13-14 NKJV

I know that times change, technology is greater than it has ever been and the younger generations are more knowledgeable than my generation, but God's Word never changes. While it's true that we may get greater revelation, greater revelation will always lead us to greater holiness and more intimacy with God. Anything that takes us farther away from His righteousness is not the true Gospel of Christ. If those who are called for this day would stop arguing about whether or not they can hold on to their sin and still go to heaven; if they would focus on preaching the Gospel, we would see the Church coming up to the heavenly level instead of being drawn down to the earthly realm (man of the dust).

We shouldn't have a need to drink alcohol if we are satisfied with the new wine of the Holy Spirit. Who cares if we can drink alcohol or not? We might be able to make it to heaven and be full of sin, but what about the little sister that is spoken of in Song of Solomon? Can the alcoholic and the drug addict make it without our witness? If we are truly friends of the Bridegroom, we willingly lay these things down for the sake of our brethren who are helpless to stand against their own addictions. These bondages are destroying families on a daily basis. It's not about right or wrong, it's about life or death. We are enraged about the sins of our nation, but we will never bring a change to our own government until we have the government of God resting upon our own shoulders.

> *"For unto us a Child is born, Unto us a Son is given; And the government will be upon His shoulder. And His name will be called Wonderful, Counselor, Mighty God, Everlasting Father, Prince of Peace."*
>
> Isaiah 9:6 nkjv

Those of us who are being prepared for this end time are required by God to set ourselves apart for His use, not for our own. I'm not talking about a title, I'm talking about a relationship with our most holy God. If we are not willing to lay our lives down for others as Christ did, we should not be in the company of the bride and the Bridegroom. It is our job to teach the bride of Christ how to be a chaste virgin, not a loose woman. We say that we are the "double portion generation," but what does that mean? I believe it is talking about the glory and holiness of God becoming greater in our lives, since the Word says we grow from glory to glory. With every generation there should be a deeper revelation of His holiness, as *"Deep calls unto deep"* (Psalm 42:7 nkjv).

> *Do you not know that you are the temple of God and that the Spirit of God dwells in you?*
>
> 1 Corinthians 3:16 nkjv

It's time to get things cleaned up in the leadership of the Church (the friends of the Bridegroom). It wasn't until King Uzziah died that Isaiah was able to see himself as an unclean man (see Isaiah 6). He could not hear the voice of God because he had sin in his life. Once his sin had been purged and taken away, he heard the voice of God calling him to go preach the Word of the Lord.

When we are looking to man for acceptance, we can't see the holiness of God. Maybe we need some things that are in our lives to die, or maybe we need to remove someone from our midst. We need to look at the fruits of the people around us. Maybe like Isaiah we are dwelling in the midst of a people of unclean lips. We need to watch what we speak and what we are listening to. From the abundance of a man's heart his mouth speaks (Luke 6:45 *paraphrased*). In other words, we are what we speak. Once again, if we are going to be a friend of the Bridegroom we must keep our lives clean so we can hear the voice of the Father.

> *Therefore, having these promises, beloved, let us cleanse ourselves from all filthiness of the flesh and spirit, perfecting holiness in the fear of God.*
> 2 Corinthians 7:1 nkjv

When we love our brother enough to lay our lives down for him, we will begin to see what we need to dethrone in our lives. We can't help others until we ourselves become overcomers. Many on the Jericho Road have been beaten up and left to die today. They need a Good Samaritan (a friend of the Bridegroom). These people have been hurt and have drawn back, but they must learn that the pain and suffering they have gone through has a much higher purpose. God's purpose for us is to be overcomers so that we can sit on the throne with Him and reign in His Kingdom on earth. All have been called to be overcomers, but all will not make it.

> *"To him that overcometh will I grant to sit with Me in My throne, even as I also overcame, and am set down with My Father in His throne."*
> Revelation 3:21 kjv

## Questions for Reflection

1. "Here He will require much more from us than just being nominal Christians. He will ask us if we are willing to eat His flesh and drink His blood." How do you respond when you sense God is requiring more of you?

   _____

   _____

2. "We need to watch what we speak and what we are listening to." Are the things you're speaking and listening to bringing you life or death? What is one way you can speak life over yourself and your family?

   _____

   _____

3. "We can't help others until we ourselves become overcomers." What have you overcome? What are you in the process of overcoming now?

   _____

   _____

# Part Two

Chapter Five

# Qualification #1: Deny Ourselves

*Then said Jesus unto his disciples, If any man will come after Me, let him deny himself, and take up his cross, and follow me. For whosoever will save his life shall lose it: and whosoever will lose his life for my sake shall find it."*

MATTHEW 16:24-25 KJV

Jesus came to the earth to fulfill His Father's will, not His own. He had a purpose, and His purpose was to be an overcomer. Jesus endured suffering, pain, and finally death. He cried out to His Father, *"If it be thy will, take this cup from me"* (Luke 22:42 *paraphrased*). But God's will was that He would be our sacrifice, so Jesus suffered the pain of the Cross for us. As God Himself and the Son of God, He chose to come to earth as a man, so He felt the same things and had the same temptations we do, but was without sin. Throughout His life, He continually chose to be an overcomer to teach us how to overcome. He laid down His life so that we could live. Denying ourselves means that we give up our rights, our desires, and our opinions, and commit our will to God's will. Our destiny lies within our obedience to the Father.

Every time God requires something from my old Adam nature that I don't want to give up because I think I have the right to keep it, He reminds me of a conversation that I had with Him when I was a very young convert. I told Him that I wanted Him to be my daddy because I'd never had a dad to raise me and love me, or even correct me. Because of this, I became a heathen but I wanted to change. All my life I'd thought that if my dad hadn't died when I was only five years old, I would have turned out differently. Of course, there is no way to know that for certain. But that night I gave God permission to do whatever He needed to do to make me a woman that He could be proud of. I really didn't know what I was asking.

Throughout my forty two years of serving God I have endured some difficult seasons. Even though it has been hard at times, I know that everything I have gone through has only been to make me like Him. If we have been birthed into the Kingdom of God, we are born in His likeness. That means we are born again with His seed so we can become the image of the Father. I know there are times when we don't act like Him, but if we have His heart we won't have a desire to do evil or to hurt others. We bear fruit that can only come from the Spirit. What is born of flesh is flesh and what is born of Spirit is spirit (John 3:6 *paraphrased*).

> *And as we have borne the image of the man of dust, we shall also bear the image of the heavenly man.*
>
> 1 CORINTHIANS 15:49 NKJV

Many of the things that we go through are the dealings of God upon our lives. As we walk through our trials, whatever they may be, we find that in the end we are able to help someone else. If we are called as John the Baptist was, to be a friend of the Bridegroom, we will go through much fire to be prepared for this day. Many throughout the Word of God have gone through great tribulation and have even given their lives to protect the Church (the bride). Jesus said if we want to find our lives, we must lose them (Luke 9:24 *paraphrased*). When Paul was full of evil, threatening to imprison and murder Christ's followers, Jesus met him on the Damascus road. As bad as he had been, one encounter with God changed his whole life. Because Paul fell in love with God, he fell in love with the bride of Christ and was willing to give his life for her. I think we all need to have an experience like Paul's so we are willing to die for the Gospel.

> *I have been crucified with Christ; it is no longer*
> *I who live but Christ lives in me.*
> GALATIANS 2:20 NKJV

## Questions for Reflection

1. "All my life I'd thought that if my dad hadn't died when I was only five years old, I would have turned out differently." What are some regrets/thought patterns you may need to surrender to God?

   _____

   _____

2. "That night I gave God permission to do whatever He needed to do to make me a woman that He could be proud of." Have you given God this kind of permission?

   _____

   _____

3. "I think we all need to have an experience like Paul's so we are willing to die for the Gospel." How far will your current level of love allow you to go?

   _____

   _____

Chapter Six

# Qualification #2: Do Not Compromise

*"For I have told him that I will judge his house forever for the iniquity which he knows, because his sons made themselves vile, and he did not restrain them."*

1 Samuel 3:13 nkjv

Hannah, a woman of God, travailed until she birthed Samuel, one of the greatest prophets in the Bible. Eli the priest was called by God to raise Samuel in the ways of God and train him in the temple. What an awesome honor that must have been! Only one thing was wrong: Eli had sin in his house. He knew his sons were evil and corrupting the temple of God. He was visited by a man giving him warning about his sons bringing sin into the temple. But Eli honored his sons more than he honored God and would not correct them. Finally, God brought judgment on the house of Eli and the whole family was struck dead. Eli lost his holy seed that God had given him.

Today God is giving us spiritual sons and daughters to train for this generation, not for ourselves but for the His Kingdom. He has placed them in our houses to teach and train them in holiness and the truth of God's Word. God is getting us ready for the greatest end time revival that the world has ever known. Just as God placed Samuel with Eli to be trained, He has called the friends of the Bridegroom to train up Samuels for this day. We are to train them to hear the Word of the Lord and respond to His voice.

Isn't it funny that Samuel was only a child and could hear the Word of the Lord and Eli the priest couldn't hear Him? The ability to hear God's voice is given to the obedient, not to those who hold iniquity in their hearts.

> *The ability to hear God's voice is given to the obedient.*

We must not compromise the Word or the ways of God to the younger generation, lest we lose our seed as Eli did. When Eli fell off the log and broke his neck, I believe that it represented him losing his strength to hold his head up. In other words, he lost his ability to be head of his household or the house of God. Eli should have corrected his sons and if they did not respond to his correction, he should have removed them from their duties in the temple. The reason for such removal is to save the other people. Eli even told them, *"You make the Lord's people transgress"* (1 Samuel 2:24 NKJV).

Just about every minister I talk to is praying for revival to come to our churches and our land. God is preparing us for an end time revival that will change the whole world, not just one church. We have read about all the revivals that have taken place in the past. In recent history, many attended the Brownsville revival that lasted more than five years. But I believe the revival that is coming is one like we have never experienced. This is why it is a must that we prepare ourselves and examine our hearts. We are about to cross over to a place in the spirit realm where we have never been. Prior to a great move of God, He has always dealt very strongly with His people to repent and lay before the altar. There is also great warfare between heaven and hell. When the Brownsville revival broke out, Pastor John Kilpatrick said it took paying a price, laying down his life and pressing through with prayer. God is calling His leaders to repent first. John writes, *"God never puts revival on sale. He never discounts it. It always costs the same for every generation."*[1]

> *And Joshua said to the people, "Sanctify yourselves, for tomorrow the Lord will do wonders among you."*
> 
> JOSHUA 3:5 NKJV

## Endnotes

1. John Kilpatrick, *When the Heavens are Brass: Keys to Genuine Revival* (Shippensburg, PA: Revival Press, 1997), p.4.

## Questions for Reflection

1. "Eli honored his sons more than he honored God and would not correct them." Is there anything that you are honoring above God?

   _____

   _____

2. "Today God is giving us spiritual sons and daughters to train for this generation, not for ourselves but for His Kingdom." Do you have spiritual parents? Do you have spiritual sons and daughters? If so, how are you training them?

   _____

   _____

3. "We must not compromise the Word or the ways of God to the younger generation, lest we lose our seed as Eli did." Are there any areas where you are compromising?

   _____

   _____

## Chapter Seven

# Qualification #3: Get Delivered of Pride

*But when he was strong his heart was lifted up, to his destruction, for he transgressed against the Lord his God by entering the temple of the Lord to burn incense on the altar of incense.*

2 CHRONICLES 26:16 NKJV

King Uzziah was a man full of pride and arrogance. He started out on the right foot just like many of God's great leaders; but we know it's not about who starts the race, but rather who finishes it. It is the enduring overcomers whom God grants to sit with Him on His throne, not those who were righteous before God at some time in the past. Our ability to use the gifts of God, such as healing or the performing of great miracles, does not mean that we are right with God. It is our responsibility to step away from a loaded gun if we have a desire to kill someone, just as it is our responsibility to step away from exercising the gifts of God when we have fallen into blatant sin. The spiritual gifts can be as dangerous as a loaded gun when they are used by someone who is out of the will of God. It is wrong to use our gifts or anointing to turn people's hearts toward ourselves. Grace was given by God so that we can be forgiven for our sin, not so we can stay in it and defile the house of God like Uzziah or Eli's sons did.

I mentioned earlier how Isaiah idolized King Uzziah. Uzziah won the hearts of many because he was a brilliant man. Many today are looking for just that in a spiritual leader. But God is not looking for a brilliant man. All that pride and arrogance came from the garden where satan filled Adam and Eve's hearts with lies about what God expected from them. It was after they ate of the forbidden fruit that pride filled their hearts. Adam was brilliant before the fall, but he gave his brilliance to the devil and allowed it to be corrupted. Without God and His righteousness, there is no such good. We can make our brain a god and it may look appealing to man, but what happens when God says, *"Fool! This night your soul shall be required of you."* (Luke 12:20 NKJV)? We can fill our barns up with things of the flesh, but one day God will come and require His goods.

> **Without God and His righteousness, there is no such thing as good.**

Let's talk about King Uzziah's life and how it relates to the leaders of today. I'm not talking about just spiritual leaders in the Church; I'm also talking about the leaders of our nation, our schools and our military. As I read about Uzziah, it reminds me of what is going on in the modern world. Initially he started out as a great man. People looked up to him because he was one of the greatest kings of the Southern Kingdom. He was only sixteen years old when he became king and he reigned for fifty two years. His name actually meant "Jehovah is strength."

When King Uzziah was still very young, he overthrew all his enemies and caused the nation to become prosperous. He was so intelligent that he invented and constructed military weapons (see 2 Chronicles 26:15). He was one of the most successful kings ever. It seems as though everything he set his hand to do prospered, and he was the rock star of the day. Not only was he idolized by the young, he was also envied by other kings (see 2 Chron. 26:8).

King Uzziah was also brilliant in setting military strategies and he prepared body armor for the entire army (see 2 Chron. 26:14). Everything that he organized was successful (see 2 Chron. 26: 9-10). Is it any wonder that everyone loved him? I believe many would say that we wish we had leaders like that today. But something happened to King Uzziah after he gained from God all that he thought he could. He began to walk in his own strength, he was puffed up in his heart, and he forgot that God was responsible for his success.

When you think about a king that God was using so powerfully you might think that he would go down in history that way, but he didn't. What caused this mighty and godly man to die with such a curse?

> *A man's pride will bring him low, but the*
> *humble in spirit will retain honor.*
> PROVERBS 29:23 NKJV

King Uzziah was so filled with pride he thought he had the right to go into the temple and change the order of the holy and righteous Jehovah God; He assumed that he was superior to God. One day Uzziah got so arrogant that he decided he could enter into the temple of the Lord and burn incense, a duty reserved only for the priests. He thought his position as king gave him the right to change the order of God.

Does that remind you of our nation's leaders today? God has blessed America abundantly—but instead of giving God the glory for it, there are those in our leadership who have become prideful and arrogant, to the point of seeming to believe they are superior to God. Some have tried to change the laws of our most holy God and promote their own. Our leadership condones the very things God calls abominations. God has called them to be His friends, to bring our nation back to being a holy nation under God ("In God we trust"). Instead, some have become enemies to God and our country. This is one reason it is critical that we pray for those who hold positions in our government.

> *Woe to those who call evil good, and good evil; Who put darkness for light and light for darkness; Who put bitter for sweet, and sweet for bitter! Woe to those who are wise in their own eyes, And prudent in their own sight! Woe to men mighty at drinking wine, Woe to men valiant for mixing intoxicating drink, who justify the wicked for a bribe, and take away justice from the righteous man!*
>
> ISAIAH 5:20-23

But this is not the end of the story! There is good news! God is about to bring some of His friends into His temple who are not afraid of losing numbers or money, and who will not compromise the Word of God:

> *Azariah the priest went in after King Uzziah, and with him were eighty priests of the Lord--valiant men. And they withstood King Uzziah and said to him…"Get out of the sanctuary, for you have trespassed! You shall have no honor from the Lord."*
>
> 2 CHRONICLES 26:17-18 NKJV

King Uzziah become furious with the priest and while he was angry, leprosy broke out on his forehead. Leprosy on his forehead signified that he had lost all his authority. He then ran out of the temple. Uzziah who was once an awesome king was now just a leper. A very short eulogy was written about him: "He is a leper" (2 Chronicles 26:23). You see, it doesn't matter how much good we have done in the past; it matters what we are doing when Jesus, the Bridegroom comes at midnight. Will our lamps be filled with His oil, and will we be able to go through His door? It's time for God's true ministers to start standing up against the spirit of pride and arrogance. We must stop allowing a prestigious spirit to rule the House of God. I also believe that God is going to strike our nation with spiritual leprosy if we don't turn back to Him.

The foundation of our nation was built upon the word of God, and when man tries to destroy what God has built, God's Word will fall upon him and turn him to powder. Isaiah chapter five speaks of this very thing.

> *In the year that King Uzziah died, I saw the Lord sitting on a throne, high and lifted up, and the train of His robe filled the temple.*
> ISAIAH 6:1 NKJV

Now that Isaiah is no longer looking upon King Uzziah, his eyes have been opened. In this hour, God is calling us to turn our eyes away from our idols, look into His eyes, and have an ear to hear what He is saying. We can look at this as a representation of a new season. Things must die in one season in order to see God high and lifted up in another. Those who truly love the Bridegroom are about to enter into another dimension where we have never before walked. This is the end of time as we know it and God has saved the best for last! This is the dimension Isaiah entered into when he stopped looking for fame and prestige from man. The encounter he had with God that day caused him to hear the voice of God and be able to say, *"Here am I! Send me"* (Isaiah 6:8 NKJV).

Let's not be like King Uzziah and end up not making it into the marriage feast of the Lamb. Many are called to be friends of the Bridegroom, but we must be proven trustworthy to go into the dressing room of the King. There are awesome treasures laying on His night stand and secret stairways that we have not been allowed to see yet. Oh, I do not want to miss it after serving Him for forty- two years!

Many will miss out on that wonderful time because they've grown tired of waiting and have lost their vision and their faith in His promises. Maybe that is what happened to the five foolish virgins that didn't make it through the door. We don't know when the Bridegroom will come, only the Father knows that, but He will come back after His bride just as He has promised.

> *"Therefore you also be ready, for the Son of Man is coming at an hour you do not expect. Who then is a faithful and wise servant, whom his master made ruler over his household, to give them food in due season? Blessed is that servant whom his master, when he comes, will find so doing. Assuredly, I say to you that he will make him ruler over all his goods. But if that evil servant says in his heart, 'My master is delaying his coming', and begins to beat his fellow servants and to eat and drink with the drunkards, the master of that servant will come on a day when he is not looking for him and at an hour that he is not aware of, and will cut him in two and appoint him his portion with the hypocrites. There shall be weeping and gnashing of teeth."*
>
> (MATTHEW 24:44-51 NKJV)

## Questions for Reflection

1. "He began to walk in his own strength, he was puffed up in his heart, and he forgot that God was responsible for his success." What do you do with your successes? Who gets credit for them?

   _____

   _____

2. "Now that Isaiah is no longer looking upon King Uzziah, his eyes have been opened." Is there a King Uzziah in your life—someone you are looking upon who is clouding your vision of God?

   _____

   _____

3. "Many are called to be friends of the Bridegroom, but we must be proven trustworthy to go into the dressing room of the King." How does God know you are trustworthy?

   _____

   _____

### Chapter Eight

# Qualification #4: Have a Heart for the Poor and Hear the Cry of Our Cities

*Whoever shuts his ears to the cry of the poor will
also cry himself and not be heard.*

PROVERBS 21:13 NKJV

Throughout the Bible, we see God's heart pouring out to the poor and the needy. As I sat at my desk asking my wonderful Bridegroom to tell me what His heart's desire was for this chapter, He seemed to be delighted that I have a burden for the poor. If we want to be a friend of the Bridegroom we must have a heart for the poor. If we have no desire to feed the poor, we do not have the heart of God. As I write, I'm writing in love, not only for the poor but also for the ones the world would call rich. I thank God that He has blessed some of His people with great wealth, because without their generosity we could not care for the poor. But there are some very serious matters I want to talk about.

I am one hundred percent in favor of international missions, but sometimes it seems that God's people are more willing to hear a cry from a distant land than they are to hear the cry across the street. We must pray for our ears to be open to hear the cry of our cities. I know that God has a people with the same burden that I have for the poor in my area. I know there are friends of the Bridegroom who will come to their rescue just as Paul did when he heard the cry from the man of Macedonia. Paul's answer to this call has always stood out to me, not because of the distance he traveled, but because of the response of his heart when he heard the cry of God's people. It is important to respond to the cry that we hear. If we listen, we may hear it in our own backyards.

> *And a vision appeared to Paul in the night. A man of Macedonia stood and pleaded with him, saying, "Come over to Macedonia and help us."*
> ACTS 16:9 NKJV

God is calling intercessors to plead for their people. I believe that we can change things in our nation if we are willing to work at changing our cities.

The poor and needy are not just those who need food, but those who are in bondage to drugs, alcohol, and suffering under all forms of abuse. This kind of bondage affects families in the worst of ways. Children are often forced to forfeit their education and grow up with no self-esteem and a mentality that they can never go beyond what their parents have achieved. Unless it is broken by the power of Jesus, this generational cycle will continue to repeat itself.

The poor are also those who are poor in spirit. Everyone doesn't know the Word well enough to prosper from it. Some will read the Scripture and not know how to apply it to their own lives. Those who are more mature in the faith are instructed to teach them how to prosper (see Titus 2). God Himself said that the poor would always be with us, and it will always be our responsibility to care for them (see Matthew 26:11). I believe when we teach those who are depressed, hurting, and broken how to apply God's Word, we are caring for them in the deepest way.

A few years ago I was at a "Pray for West Virginia" conference. As I was praying, I looked up at the big map of West Virginia on the wall, and I saw fire on every county in the state. God spoke to me and said, "I am taking all of West Virginia, one county at a time." Since then, my focus has been on the counties of my state. I am probably not an apostle for the nations, but I do know that I am an interceding apostle for our state and the counties that lie within its borders.

One of the great women of the Bible, Deborah, heard the cry of her city and as a result, won the war over the enemy that had been threatening to destroy it. Deborah was a prophetess who sat under the palm tree and heard from the people. I would call her a gatekeeper of the city. Nothing went on there that she didn't know about. As she heard the cries of the people daily, she got a burden for them. She called out to Barak knowing that God had already spoken to him. Deborah began to work on the strategy of war. She asked him:

> *"Has not the Lord God of Israel commanded, 'go and deploy troops at Mount Tabor; take with you ten thousand men of the sons of Naphtali and of the sons of Zebulun; and against you I will deploy Sisera, the commander of Jabin's army, with his chariots and his multitude at the River Kishon; and I will deliver him into your hand?'"*
> 
> JUDGES 4:6-7 NKJV

When we are able to hear the cry of our cities, then and only then will we be able to hear from God concerning the strategy we need to use to help the people and win the war. If we have given ourselves to be friends of the Bridegroom, we will be willing to do whatever is necessary to overtake the enemy, regardless of where God has placed us. Because of Deborah's burden for the poor and oppressed, she was able to hear from God when it was time to go to battle for her people.

> *Then Deborah said to Barak, "Up! For this is the day in which the Lord has delivered Sisera into your hand. Has not the Lord gone out before you?" So Barak went down from Mount Tabor with ten thousand men following him.*
>
> JUDGES 4:14 NKJV

The children of Israel had once again been taken into bondage by the enemy because of their sin. Sin is always the cause of bondage whether it is to poverty, drugs, sex, or any other enslavement. Even with all our sinful choices, God, our loving Father, always has someone who is willing to yield to His call and intercede for our deliverance. When we hear the cry of our cities or nations, we are hearing the cry of Jesus for His bride. If we want to be recognized as His friends, we must drink of the cup that He drank from for the world. It means complete surrender of our lives, no matter what God may ask of us.

To ask a man to sell all that he has and give it to the poor is a hard saying for anyone (Mark 10:21-22 *paraphrased*). The Bible says that man walked away sorrowful; he wasn't willing to do what was asked. God may not ask you to sell all that you have, but what is it that He *is* asking of you? Mary, the mother of Jesus, told the friends at the wedding in Cana: *"Whatever He says to you, do it"* (John 2:5 NKJV).

# Qualification #4: Have a Heart for the Poor and Hear the Cry of Our Cities | 57

God is calling a people out of a people and training them to establish His Millennial Kingdom on earth—a people who have given Him total permission to rule and reign in and through them. We need to totally relinquish our rights and give Him full permission to govern our lives as He chooses. I, myself, want to be able to say to Him, "Yes Sir, whatever you say!" However, I know there will always be times when I will struggle, and maybe walk away sorrowfully when God asks something difficult of me, simply because my flesh needs to die more. There is a great battle going on in the heavens right now over the Church because the sons of God are about to be birthed as one new man (see Revelation 12:1-5). We must be ready when Jesus comes to take His bride.

*We must be ready when Jesus comes to take His bride.*

## Questions for Reflection

1. "We must pray for our ears to be open to hear the cry of our cities." Has God given you a burden for the area where you live?

   _____

   _____

2. "Even with all our sinful choices, God, our loving Father always has someone who is willing to yield to His call and intercede for our deliverance." Who are you interceding for?

   _____

   _____

3. "God may not ask you to sell all that you have, but what is it that He *is* asking of you?"

   _____

   _____

## Chapter Nine

# Qualification #5: Be Militant

*No one engaged in warfare entangles himself with the affairs of this life, that he may please him who enlisted him as a soldier.*

2 Timothy 2:4 nkjv

There has never been a more violent battle between satan and the Church than there is in this end time. If we are going to be in the company of the Bridegroom, we must be militant. This is satan's last try before Jesus comes, so he is releasing his best demons from hell. The dirtiest demon he is using today is the one that comes to destroy the family. He is causing women to murder their own unborn babies and calling it, "the right to my own body;" pornography sales are at an all-time high; and young children are being bought and sold as sex slaves.

The friends of the Bridegroom must not be afraid of the intimidating demons from hell; their job is to keep the bride of Christ clean and pure for her wedding day. But they must do this in God's order. In Joel's army, we are told that the soldiers *"do not break ranks"* (Joel 2:7 NKJV).

Let's look at the importance of following God's strategies by keeping ourselves in order. Just as a good soldier guards his camp from the enemy, Aaron was supposed to be keeping rank while Moses was away. He was to watch over the camp, but as Scripture tells us, he didn't do a very good job. Instead of protecting the camp, Aaron helped the people make a golden calf to worship and caused a perverted spirit to come in. If we are really going to keep the bride clean, friends of the Bridegroom must keep rank.

> *God is calling an army to fight the devil until he surrenders.*

When I look at the hyper-grace message being preached today, I see the enemy using it to turn the younger generation away from the righteousness of God. I believe in grace one hundred percent. I could not be saved without it, but what I don't believe is that we can be in outright sin and perversion and still be right with God. God is calling an army that is not afraid to stand up for what they believe in and fight the devil until he surrenders.

In Jude we find that God is warning His people about being blinded to what is going on around them. Jude seems to be very upset about men who have crept into their assembly unnoticed. He warns them that these men are trying to turn their hearts from God and His righteousness. He warns them of the judgment of God that has even fallen upon the angels that did not keep their place in holiness. They have been put into darkness and everlasting chains. Finally, he warns them that these people have gone the way of Cain, have run greedily in the error of Balaam for profit, and are in the rebellion of Korah.

Now let's talk about Cain, Balaam and Korah. Who were these horrible men that Jude was talking about? I believe they were not just men, but demonic spirits that had crept in by way of sin. When the Church gets apathetic, it is like poison gas seeping into a building and putting everyone to sleep. With their minds blinded, they are vulnerable to believing lies. This is why we must seek God like never before. Spirits will come in and infiltrate the Church if we are not doing warfare.

**Cain** represents a religious, jealous spirit that killed Abel. When God received Abel's offering and not his, he got so angry and jealous that he killed his brother. God would not receive Cain's offering because it was from the ground and not a blood sacrifice. In other words, it came from his own sinful flesh. He was trying to do the same thing that his parents had done when they covered their sin with fig leaves. Cain was full of pride and would not ask God to forgive him. There are people today who get very angry at Christians because they won't change the Word of God to please them. God has never and will never accept an offering of sin. What God *will* do is accept us while we are still in our sin ... and change us.

When God came into the garden looking for Adam and Eve, they had nothing on but fig leaves that were taken from the ground. They had lost the Glory that had covered them. The ground represents the flesh that we were made from. The lamb represents Jesus the Lamb, who shed His blood to cover our sin. God will not accept an unholy sacrifice no matter how much we preach about grace. If we are looking for a way to live in blatant sin and make it to heaven, we need to question whether or not we are really saved. Maybe we have gone the way of Cain. Maybe we would rather kill our brother than repent and allow the blood of Jesus to save us and change us (see Genesis 4:8).

**Balaam** represents the spirit of error. Balaam was a prophet of God. Those whom he blessed were blessed, and those whom he cursed were cursed (Numbers 22:6 *paraphrased*). The Moabites tried to deceive Balaam into going with them and cursing God's people, but God made it clear to him that he was not to do this (see Numbers 22: 12). Now this was a great test for Balaam, as it is for us today. Balaam refused the first time, but the princes of Moab came back a second time, offering him great honor (see Numbers 22:17). Would he listen to God or the spirit that was enticing him?

Here is where we get to sometimes; we want to obey God, but we give in to offers of honor, riches, and other things that make our flesh feel good. Sometimes we entertain these thoughts long enough that God allows us to have what we want. I've seen this many times when a person wants to marry someone, but God has not given His permission. If they go ahead without God's blessing, it ends up in disaster.

In Numbers 22:20, God told Balaam to go with the men if they came again, only because He'd lifted His protection off Balaam and was allowing him to do what *his* heart wanted. God knew those men would be back! He always knows our hearts and He always gives us opportunities to have them tested. Because some people want to hear a lie so they can have what their flesh wants and not feel conviction, God Himself will allow those to fall into deception.

> *And for this reason God will send them strong delusion, that they should believe the lie.*
> 2 Thessalonians 2:11 NKJV

If we are going to be soldiers in the Lord's end time army, we will be tested to see if we will sell Him out for a price. We need to ask ourselves, "Is there a price that I would sell out for?" If I can't be bought for twenty dollars, but I can be bought for a million dollars, my heart is not right with God. Our leaders in the pulpit today have been offered a lot to give in to the devil. This is the day of prosperity for God's people, but we have to make sure we don't go the way of Balaam to get it.

> *For false christs and false prophets will rise and show great signs and wonders to deceive, if possible, even the elect.*
> MATTHEW 24:24 NKJV

The next spirit we must watch out for is the spirit of **Korah**, which is the spirit of rebellion. In Numbers 16, Korah and his followers rose up against Moses with pride and rebellion. In doing this, Korah imparted rebellion into the hearts of 250 men. When people are following us, whatever we are not willing to be delivered from will find its way into their hearts. There must always be a circumcision of the heart.

Though Korah and his followers had talents, gifts, and power, Jude called them dreamers (see Jude 1:8). Talents, gifts, and power are not qualifications for leadership. God sets men in headship positions because they have the heart of the Father. Man cannot choose his position in the Kingdom. Rebellion against God's order will always cause death in one way or another. In the end of the Israelites' rebellion, 14,700 people died by the plague, not including those who were swallowed up by the ground. We will be swallowed up by the ground (our flesh) if we enter into rebellion against authority.

Acts of rebellion not only affect the present generation, but also those who will come after us. In Ezekiel 44, we see the sons of Zadok being chosen to enter into the holy place, while the Levites were not allowed to minister to the Lord because of a previous generation's rebellion.

> *"They shall enter My sanctuary, and they shall come near My table to minister to Me, and they shall keep My charge."*
>
> EZEKIEL 44:16 NKJV

> *"Now say to the rebellious, to the house of Israel, 'Thus says the Lord God: "O house of Israel, let Us have no more of all your abominations. When you brought in foreigners, uncircumcised in heart and uncircumcised in flesh, to be in My sanctuary to defile it—My house—and when you offered My food, the fat and the blood, then they broke My covenant because of all your abominations."'*
>
> EZEKIEL 44:6-7 NKJV

God did not hold the foreigners responsible for the defilement of His house. It was because of the Israelites' abominations that these foreigners broke God's covenant. Friends of the Bridegroom are called to keep God's sanctuary clean and to teach others to honor His presence. We must be careful to always stay submitted to our Lord and not give the least consideration to rebellion in our lives.

God is raising up one of the greatest armies that has ever been on the earth. It is an army comprised of the end time friends of the Bridegroom—an army that will not be overthrown. As I began writing this book, I asked God what this army was and who these friends are. Are they not the bride? Will they not be part of the bride of Christ that will sit with Him on His throne?

This is the vision God gave me: I saw the radiant bride of Christ, dressed in her white gown and all His glory. As I looked at her, I began to see great warriors coming out of her by the thousands. They were dressed in battle array with swords of fire in their hands. The expressions on their faces told me that they were not backing up for any devil, no matter what form he might take. It was an awesome sight to see the mighty warriors within the bride!

> *Blow the trumpet in Zion, and sound an alarm in My holy mountain!*
> JOEL 2:1 NKJ

The following is the interpretation of that vision: The bride, of course, was the Church. She was dressed in a white wedding gown without blemish. By this I knew she was in her end-time dress of maturity. God was showing me how much the bride had grown, even though many think she is on her way down, including the devil. He explained to me, "She has been growing from glory to glory, and as she grows through every season, a greater part of who I Am will come out of her."

In this current season, the warrior Spirit of God is coming out of her because that is what is needed in this end time to battle the spirits of deception that are coming. God said, "I am calling My warriors out of her, that they might rise up as a mighty army on the earth and declare war against the evil one that is bragging in hell that he will kill the Church, My bride. My Church will always remain strong and the gates of hell will not prevail against her. When it is over, everything that has come out of her will return back into her, and we shall then sit on My throne and she shall be called 'My Bride, the Overcomer!'"

The second chapter of Joel talks about this mighty army. There are qualifications for being in this army that we need to meet if we are going to do warfare for the Kingdom. These people are not just churchgoers, nor are they looking for a place to hide from the great and terrible day of the Lord. They are a people who have purposefully chosen to come into unity that they might bless the Kingdom of God. This war is not just about casting out a few demons; this war is about warring against the kingdom of darkness.

**What is God looking for in these end-time warriors?** (Joel 2:7-9 NKJV).

- They climb over the walls (vs.7)
- Everyone marches in formation (vs.7)
- They do not break ranks (vs.7)
- They do not push one another (vs.8)
- Everyone marches in his own column (vs.8)
- They lunge between the weapons (vs.8)
- They are not cut down (vs.8)
- They run to and fro in the city (vs.9)
- They run on the wall (vs.9)
- They climb into the houses (vs.9)
- They enter at the windows like a thief (vs.9)

> *The earth quakes before them, the heavens tremble; the sun and moon grow dark, and the stars diminish their brightness. The Lord gives voice before His army, For His camp is very great; For strong is the One who executes His word. For the day of the Lord is great and very terrible; who can endure it?*
>
> JOEL 2:10-11 NKJV

This army will walk in step with the Lord and will do things in time with Him. They will walk in perfect unity and not fight amongst themselves. They will do what they have been trained to do, in the ways they've been trained to do it. They will work together as a network to bring a great harvest, and they each will operate in their own God-given anointing for His Kingdom. This army of the Lord will not compromise the Word to get fame or riches for themselves. This is why the devil will not be able to overpower them.

Just think, all this power and glory is inside the bride of Christ, and the devil calls her weak! The bride *will* be ready for her Beloved when He comes. She will be wearing a garment of righteousness without spot, blemish, or wrinkle.

> *I will greatly rejoice in the Lord, my soul shall be joyful in my God; For He has clothed me with the garments of salvation, He has covered me with the robe of righteousness, As a bridegroom decks himself with ornaments, And as a bride adorns herself with her jewels. For as the earth brings forth its bud, As the garden causes the things that are sown in it to spring forth, So the Lord God will cause righteousness and praise to spring forth before all the nations.*
>
> ISAIAH 61:10-11 NKJV

The time spoken of by Isaiah will be a time of greatness and the manifestation of the power of God. Signs, wonders, and miracles will occur, not just in certain places, but in all places where the name of Jesus and His Word are being honored. His Word tells us not to say *"lo, here is Christ or there He is,"* for the Kingdom of God is within us (Luke 17:21 *paraphrased*). His parousia (manifest presence) is in our midst, calling us to battle against the demons of this world so the true revival can come to the whole earth. We in the Body of Christ must stop fighting each other and come together in unity if we are going to be the overcomers that He speaks about in Revelation 3:20-22.

## Questions for Reflection

1. "Maybe we would rather kill our brother than repent and allow the blood of Jesus to save us and change us." Are you harboring jealousy or resentment toward anyone? If so, will you repent and allow Jesus to change this?

   _____

   _____

2. "We want to obey God, but we give in to offers of honor, riches, and other things that make our flesh feel good." What are some things that try to draw you away from God?

   _____

   _____

3. "Whatever we are not willing to be delivered of, will find its way into the hearts of those who look up to us." Are there any areas of rebellion in your life?

   _____

   _____

Chapter Ten

# Qualification #6: Have a Heart for Prayer and Worship

*"Men always ought to pray and not lose heart."*
LUKE 18:1 NKJV

Whatever we do, we must spend time with God in order to know His heart. Can you imagine going to battle and not getting any instructions from your commanding officer? It probably wouldn't be long until you would be defeated by the enemy. The same is true with being a friend of the Bridegroom. If we don't pray, how can we know His plan for the Church? Prayer is where we gain access to the throne room. If we don't have a heart to pray, how can we do any kind of warfare for the Kingdom of God?

The friends of the Bridegroom are also intercessors, sometimes called the gatekeepers and the watchmen on the wall. God is calling intercessors up from the wilderness and into the light to do warfare against the powers of darkness in this end time. They are a vital part of the great and mighty end time army.

Nehemiah is an Old Testament friend of the Bridegroom who never came down off the wall until the job was finished. He prayed, he fasted, he interceded, and he mourned. And Nehemiah had one quality that we all need: perseverance. No matter how fierce the battle gets, the friends of the Bridegroom must stay on the wall where God has placed them.

As cupbearer to the king, Nehemiah's job was to taste the king's wine before it was served to him, in case it had been poisoned. I'm sure he was getting paid well because he was willing to give his life for the king. It sounds like Nehemiah was pretty comfortable in the palace until he realized that God's people were in great distress and needed his help.

Nehemiah heard from one of the brethren that the Jews who had been released from captivity were in great distress and the wall of Jerusalem was broken down. He tells us, *"So it was, when I heard these words, that I sat down and wept, and mourned for many days; I was fasting and praying before the God of heaven"* (Nehemiah 1:4 NKJV).

It's time for us to rise from our sleep as Nehemiah did, and receive the burden of the Lord for His people. Those who are God's friends will have a burden for the Church (His bride). Just as Jerusalem's wall was broken down and needed to be repaired, so is the Church in need of repair today.

Nehemiah was clearly not thinking of himself; his burden was for God's people. He couldn't sleep or eat because of the burden he carried. Just as Nehemiah mourned and prayed for Jerusalem, we need to hear God's cry for His people. You see, there are still portions of the bride who are lost in the world and in great bondage as the Jews were in Nehemiah's day.

We must pray for revival so the bride of Christ can be made complete before His coming. It's almost midnight and the Bridegroom is standing at the door, knocking. Those who will hear are hearing the cry, *"Behold, the Bridegroom cometh; go ye out to meet Him"* (Matthew 25:6 KJV).

It is a fearful thing to know that He is coming soon and many will not go through the door. Some will be left behind, just as they were in Noah's day. Friends of the Bridegroom, you must not give up because of discouragement or weariness! Stay on the wall and persevere until He comes. God is sharing His secrets with His friends at this time.

> *After these things I looked, and behold, a door standing open in heaven. And the first voice which I heard was like a trumpet speaking with me, saying, "Come up here, and I will show you things which must take place after this."*
>
> REVELATION 4:1 NKJV

In the book of Acts, prayer was so powerful in the prayer meeting at Mary's house that it reached right into the jail where Peter was bound in chains and watched by the prison guards. Prayer broke off the chains and enabled him to walk right past the guards and leave the prison (see Acts 12:5-11).

There are people in bondage, bound in chains by satan, and guarded by his demons. They are waiting on intercessors to rise up and pray for their release. Many of these people are fivefold ministers who have fallen into the hands of satan; some into sexual immorality, some into drugs and alcohol, and others who have just grown discouraged and lost their vision. It doesn't matter why they are there. What matters is that they are part of the company of the bride and they are needed to help bring her into maturity! The only way they are going to be set free is if an army of prayer warriors begins to intercede.

We are on the verge of birthing a revival like we have never before seen on the earth. It is time for the intercessors to bear down like they have never done in times past. Bearing down is like going into face to face combat with the enemy: you're in, there is no turning back; the heat is on. Some are going to win, but some will lose this battle. We can only win this battle with the weapon of prayer.

> *For we do not wrestle against flesh and blood, but against principalities, against powers, against the rulers of darkness of this age, against spiritual hosts of wickedness in the heavenly places.*
> EPHESIANS 6:12 NKJV

Intercessors are now being trained for this kind of battle. End-time interceding prayer warriors will be able to run into the battle and never turn back, no matter what they may see in front of them. They become war horses in the army of the Lord. If it seems as though the battle before you is greater than the battle behind you, it is. God is training you for the Millennial Kingdom!

There are twenty-four-hour prayer groups springing up all over the world. These prayer warriors are those whom God is calling out of a people to war for the Bride of Christ. For this reason, they must be trained and tested by the Holy Spirit. Remember, only those who can be trusted can be in the dressing room of the Bride and the Bridegroom. There are things that go on in the dressing room that everyone doesn't get to see.

I remember my wedding day as the most exciting time of my life. Only the ones I was closest to were allowed to come in where I was preparing to walk down the aisle. I would never have allowed strangers to see me dressing. In that room, we discussed things that were only shared between friends.

I also asked my husband what went on in his side of the dressing room and he said, "I talked to my best friend about how in love I was with you, and that I knew the Father had chosen you for me. I told him that you were not like any of the other women I had known before. I even told him that this would be the most exciting night of my life." He then told me, "You know, I would not have said that to just anyone because I would have felt like I was sharing my bride with someone who really didn't care. When my best friend/best man stood with me waiting for my bride to come down the aisle, I knew that he was so happy for me and not jealous of me. He gave up anything he might have wanted to do that day to make my day wonderful." That's a friend!

Like Nehemiah, Hannah had the perseverance of an interceding prayer warrior. She had a call to birth Samuel, one of God's greatest prophets, but it was not easy for her. She went through a lot to get her answer, but she never gave up. Hannah's faith was tested as to whether or not she would be able to persevere for what God wanted birthed into the world. Even though Hannah knew she should be able to conceive, for some reason she was hindered, but that baby was moving inside of her before she even got pregnant. Hannah knew if she prayed long enough something would happen.

When we are praying and believing for something, there are always different spirits that try to talk us out of believing God. Hannah had a husband who asked, "Am I not better to you than ten sons?" (1 Samuel 1:8 NKJV). In other words, "Why can't you just settle for what you can see and feel?" We are always tempted to settle for what is in front of us. The priest, Eli, thought she was drunk

*When we pray, spirits will always try to talk us out of believing God.*

and told her to put away her wine. Apparently he had never seen anyone pray in the Spirit before! Religious spirits will come at us when we are wrestling in prayer. The ones that say, "There must be something wrong with you; look how ugly you are."

And watch for that spirit of Peninnah that will provoke you to jealousy because she has given birth to many children, while you have yet to birth even one. This spirit will try to make you feel as if you are not pleasing to God. Hannah prayed until she birthed. She didn't care what the voices around her were saying; she believed God.

There is an end time corporate body that is birthing a very special son that can only be born at the end of time. He is called "the one new man." This is when Jews and Gentiles are one in Him.

> *"That they all may be one, as You, Father, are in Me, and I in You; that they also may be one in Us, that the world may believe that You sent Me. And the glory which You gave Me I have given them, that they may be one just as We are one."*
> JOHN 17:21-22 NKJV

The Father's desire is that we become one as He and His Son Jesus are one. This is why God is calling those who will pray and turn from their wicked ways, promising that He will hear them (see 2 Chronicles 7:14). The Father's heart is to have a Bride for His Son who is pure and without blemish. There are people who are willing to lay down their lives in prayer to become friends of the Bridegroom. Many are being called to the company of the Bride and Groom for this day.

The day is coming very soon that everyone will be in one perfect Body and there will be no more warfare.

*In whom the whole building being fitted together,
grows into a holy temple in the Lord.*

EPHESIANS 2:21 NKJV

*For He Himself is our peace, who has made both one, and has broken down the middle wall of separation, having abolished in His flesh the enmity, that is, the law of commandments contained in ordinances, so as to create in Himself one new man from the two, thus making peace, and that He might reconcile them both to God in one body through the cross, thereby putting to death the enmity.*

EPHESIANS 2:14-16 NKJV

## Questions for Reflection

1. "Friends of the Bridegroom, you must not give up because of discouragement or weariness!" How do you battle discouragement and weariness in your own life?

   _____

   _____

2. "She didn't care what the voices around her were saying; she believed God." In what area do you need to ignore the voices around you and press in to believe God for your promise?

   _____

   _____

3. "The Father's desire is that we become one as He and His Son, Jesus are one." What do you do to promote unity in your local body of believers?

   _____

   _____

# Part Three

## Chapter Eleven

# Those Who Represent the Friends of the Bridegroom

*And the Scripture was fulfilled which says, "Abraham believed God, and it was accounted to him for righteousness." And he was called the friend of God.*

JAMES 2:23 NKJV

Abraham is one of many believers throughout the Bible who represent the friends of the Bridegroom. God called Abraham His friend because he was righteous and he believed God. Abraham and these other friends have been called out because of their willingness to be obedient.

Let's look at some of the reasons that Abraham qualified to be called a friend of God.

- Abraham was totally surrendered to God.
- When tested, he was willing to give his own son—the very thing that God had promised him, and the thing he loved most.

- He was not a friend of the world; he separated himself from it.
- He did not compromise with the king of Sodom when he was offered money; he couldn't be bought.
- His whole heart was committed to God.
- He never questioned when God told him to move from his land with no indication of where he was going.
- He trusted God with everything he had, including his future.

Like Abraham, our obedience must be tested before God can trust us with His bride. Apart from such testing, we never know what could make us compromise. As we mature in obedience, the Father will trust us to prepare the bride for her wedding day.

When Abraham's son, Isaac was old enough to be married, Abraham knew he would need someone whom he could trust to find a bride for him. Although his name is not mentioned in the story, I believe that it was Eleazar, the oldest servant in the house of Abraham.

Remember, this was the son that God Himself spoke into Abraham's loins. Abraham and Sarah were both the same as dead, meaning they were too old to have any live seed in them, when they conceived Isaac. He was a special child that would carry the promise of the innumerable descendants promised to Abraham.

I consider Abraham's servant to be a friend of the Bridegroom and a type of a friend of God. He must have been a very special servant to be allowed to choose a bride for Isaac and make sure she arrived safely at her destination. The servant never exalted himself to her. He spoke only of her beloved and caused her to fall in love with Isaac before she ever saw him. He could have turned her heart to himself when he came to her parent's home to ask for her hand in marriage to Isaac. After all, he came bearing gifts for the entire household.

We have servants of God today who go into the church with gifts, not to cause the bride to fall more deeply in love with the Bridegroom, but to get her to follow after him or her. God is looking for friends that He can trust to bring His Bride home to Him just as Abraham trusted Eleazar to bring Rebekah to Isaac.

Abraham told Eleazar exactly what signs to look for in choosing his son's bride, and the servant never added or took away from what Isaac's father had told him. God is also looking for the same thing in those whom He has called to equip His bride in this hour. When we are called into fivefold ministry, we should only say what God is saying to His bride and we should never entice her to look at us.

Like Abraham's servant, we should never change the pattern that God has given us for His bride. There are signs that we are to look for as to whether or not she is truly His bride, and not an impersonator. If we are only seeking our own gain, we probably won't know the difference.

I'm sure that Rebekah was not the only woman in the city drawing water, since the servant made sure he came at a time when the women were all drawing water for the evening (see Genesis 24:11). He could have easily pursued any of those women, but that is not why he was there. He had one thing in mind and that was to get the woman his master had instructed him to find.

As friends of the Bridegroom, there are signs that we are to look for in the bride. If these signs are not there, maybe we are trying to lead someone to the marriage feast who is nothing more than a pretty woman hanging around the well, or a Jezebel trying to get something for free.

Here are some of the servant's qualifications:

- He was faithful and a good steward over his master's goods (vs.10)
- He knew timing and strategy (vs.11)
- He prayed for confirmation; he didn't just make a wild guess (vs.14)
- His heart was to please his master, not himself (vs.14)
- He must have had discernment to know that she was a virgin (vs.16)
- He tested her before taking her to Isaac (vs.20)
- He didn't give her gifts until he was sure he had God's approval, and that she was the bride (vs.21)
- He respected her household (vs.31)

There is so much more that could be brought out about this faithful servant to prove that he was truly a friend. One thing I do want to highlight is his honesty.

In Genesis 24:8, Abraham told the servant that if he couldn't find a bride for Isaac, he would be released from the oath they had made. The servant could have returned and told Abraham that he couldn't find the woman, and he would have been released and probably lived very comfortably on Abraham's provision for the rest of his life. But this servant was not deceitful in any way. He was a man of honor and he laid down his life for his master. This is what God is looking for in His friends whom He has called to watch over His bride.

As I said before, we must watch out for impostors. Not everyone who says, "Lord, Lord," is part of the bride. If they are not wearing the wedding garment of righteousness, they are not part of the wedding feast and cannot be part of the preparation of the bride of Christ.

> *"Then he said to his servants, 'the wedding is ready, but those who were invited were not worthy. Therefore go into the highways and as many as you find, invite to the wedding;' But when the king came in to see the guests, he saw a man there who did not have on a wedding garment. So he said to him, 'Friend, how did you come in here without a wedding garment?' And he was speechless. "Then the king said to the servants, 'Bind him hand and foot, take him away, and cast him into outer darkness; there will be weeping and gnashing of teeth.' For many are called, but few are chosen."*
> MATTHEW 22:8-9;12-14 NKJV

We as friends of the Bridegroom (ones called to equip the bride) must watch out for those who are in defiance and rebellion against God within the church. We are sometimes tempted to look the other way, even though we discern that a person is not of our fold. The reason? They are sometimes prominent people who pay large tithes or maybe we don't have enough people in the church to accomplish our vision. The reasons can be many, including our own self-esteem. No matter what the reason, we leaders are called to watch over the bride of Christ. As we read the above parable, we can see that the king was not pleased with the man who had no wedding garment on. Let's look a little more closely at this.

First of all, we see that the king had prepared a wedding feast and invited people to come, but they had excuses and were not willing to attend. He sent the servants several times, but none of the people came. The king, being very upset by this, decided to invite anyone who wanted to come, no matter who they were. The banqueting room was full. It was now the hour for the king to come and inspect the guests to see which of those had been obedient to the rules of the wedding party.

When he came in, he saw a man participating in the feast without a wedding garment on, an insult to the king and his son. If you notice, the king called him 'friend' just as Jesus called Judas 'friend.' I believe the king was waiting for him to humble himself and repent, but the man did not.

It's amazing how God comes in and begins to shake and sift the people after a revival or after our church grows in attendance. Wolves in sheep's clothing creep in to the Church unaware. We must watch out for this during times of church growth. We are to use our nets to draw in many, but all fish are not good.

Jesus makes this point in other parables. In the parable of the wheat, the wheat is not all good grain. Some is chaff and must be separated when the harvest season comes. In the same way, gold is not pure until the dross is separated from it. We must be proven by both inward *and* outward holiness.

> **We must be proven by both inward *and* outward holiness.**

The reason the king got so upset with this man at the wedding was because he was full of enmity and pride, with no intention to change. God gives us all a time and season to see that we are wretched, miserable, poor, blind, and naked (see Revelation 3:17). When that time has passed, He will come and sift us as wheat. The guests represent ones who come to church but will take no part in worship and honor to the Bridegroom, God's Son. They are spots and blemishes while they feast with you (see 2 Peter 2:13). We must have grace and faith to deliver us from the love of the world, not to give us permission to be a partaker of it.

If we are called to leadership, we need know who the friends are in the banqueting room. We need to remember that this is His party, not ours. We don't get to pick and choose what we put on, just as the man at the wedding feast did not get to choose what he would wear. The servants passed out the same kind of garment to everyone who came. If the leaders don't know what the garment is supposed to look like, how will the heathen who are coming into the revival ever know? We all must be dressed in the same kind of garment.

> *I will greatly rejoice in the Lord, My soul shall be joyful in my God; For He has clothed me with the garments of salvation, He has covered me with the robe of righteousness, As a bridegroom decks himself with ornaments, And as a bride adorns herself with her jewels.*
>
> ISAIAH 61:10 NKJV

> *Now Joshua was clothed with filthy garments, and was standing before the Angel. Then He answered and spoke to those who stood before Him, saying, "Take away the filthy garments from him." And to him He said, "See, I have removed your iniquity from you, and I will clothe you with rich robes."*
>
> ZECHARIAH 3:3-4 NKJV

> *"He who overcomes shall be clothed in white garments, and I will not blot out his name from the Book of Life; but I will confess his name before My Father and before His angels."*
>
> REVELATION 3:5 NKJV

> *And to her it was granted to be arrayed in fine linen, clean and bright, for the fine linen is the righteous acts of the saints.*
>
> REVELATION 19:8 NKJV

You will find in the Scriptures that we must be clothed in the garments of righteousness. We cannot wear our own garments, for they are filthy rags (see Isaiah 64:6). We must be clothed in the righteousness of God. When God came into the garden looking for Adam and Eve, He found that they had clothed themselves with fig leaves. The first thing He required of them was that they confess their sin. He then killed an animal and made garments for them. Something had to give its life. A sacrifice had to be given. That's what Jesus was for us. If we are not wearing garments of righteousness, we have no place at the wedding.

There is not a different garment for every generation, nor is there one for the rich and another for the poor. The King is sending out His call right now, inviting anyone who wants to come to the banquet to come. Behold, the Bridegroom cometh!

## Questions for Reflection

1. "He never questioned when God told him to move from his land with no indication of where he was going." How do you respond when you don't understand what God is doing?

   _____

   _____

2. "We should only say what God is saying to His bride and we should never entice her to look at us." Do you intentionally point people to Jesus, or do you try to keep some glory for yourself?

   _____

   _____

3. "Wolves in sheep's clothing creep in to the Church unaware." Are you able to discern those who are seeking to harm the Body of Christ?

   _____

   _____

*If we are not wearing garments of righteousness, we have no place at the wedding.*

## Chapter Twelve

# A Friend of God's Jewish Bride

> *Esther had not revealed her people or family, for Mordecai had charged her not to reveal it. And every day Mordecai paced in front of the court of the women's quarters, to learn of Esther's welfare and what was happening to her.*
>
> ESTHER 2:10-11 NKJV

In the book of Esther we find there is a very important part of the story that is easy to overlook. Behind the scenes, Esther had a cousin named Mordecai who was working on her behalf. Mordecai was up during the night pacing back and forth, praying for her. His main concern was to keep Esther safe because he knew there was an enemy in the palace. If he didn't watch over her, the enemy could learn of her plan to expose Haman, and her people would not be set free. Esther is a type of the Church, the bride of Christ, and Mordecai is a type of the friend of the Bridegroom. Friends of the Bridegroom take great care of the bride, to make sure her mission is accomplished and that she makes it to the throne with her King.

The devil has been working in the Church for many years, deceiving and lying, claiming the rights to the throne of the King. But the bride is almost ready to show just how powerful she really is. The bride has been in preparation since God clothed Adam and Eve in the garden. But what the devil doesn't know is that she and her Bridegroom have friends working right under his nose. The devil has lied about his power long enough; it's time to lead the bride to the throne!

Mordecai loved Esther like his own daughter, and he was willing to give his life for her. He knew that she had a job to do for the Jews, and that it was the heart of God for her to deliver His people. Knowing that the Jewish race was God's chosen people, Esther was willing to die for them. She went so far as to say, *"If I perish I perish"* (Esther 4:16 NKJV).

The Jews represent the people of God who are in bondage to the enemy (Haman) within them. God is preparing the bride (Church) to expose the enemy and set His people free, just as Esther did.

I believe that Mordecai had prayed for years, waiting for just the right time until Haman (the enemy) would be exposed. He took Esther as his own daughter when her mother and father died. Perhaps he knew that God was preparing her for that very time.

> *"Yet who knows whether you have come to the kingdom for such a time as this?"*
> ESTHER 4:14 NKJV

As we see the Church as a type in Esther, we see how the enemy has attempted to overthrow her. He is working today like never before to kill her and to entice her to lie with strange lovers. The world is trying to get her to exchange her holiness for filthy garments. But praise God, there are Mordecais who are watching over her and interceding for her until she can stand before the King in all her glory! That is a friend of the Bridegroom, the one who will lay his life down for the bride.

> *When Mordecai learned all that had happened, he tore his clothes and put on sackcloth and ashes, and went out into the midst of the city. He cried out with a loud and bitter cry.*
> ESTHER 4:1

I want to briefly mention Queen Vashti and what she represents, and why she was thrown out of the palace. On the seventh day (indicating the end time), the king prepared a feast and sent for Vashti to join him dressed in the attire that he loved. Queen Vashti refused to come when the king called for her. She rebelled against the king, and she wanted no intimacy with him. Vashti represents a spirit of rebellion within the Church and she must be thrown out. Remember the man that we read about in Matthew 22, the one at the wedding feast without a wedding garment? The king bound him hand and foot and threw him into outer darkness.

Our wonderful King is calling the Church to come to an intimate place with Him, dressed in the robe of righteousness that He has prepared for her. Those who will not bow because of rebellion will not be attending the wedding feast. God's bride will have attributes of Queen Esther—she will come when the King calls, and she will dress in the apparel that He chooses for her.

Mordecai stayed in the palace for years, not being recognized for who he really was. He was willing to wait for the right time and he knew when it had arrived, as he told Esther, *"For such a time as this"* (Esther 4:14). Are we willing to stay where God has placed us to help equip the bride and protect her, for such a time as this? Are you a friend of the Bridegroom or one who refuses to obey the King when He calls?

## Questions for Reflection

1. "Queen Vashti refused to come when the king called for her. She rebelled against the king, and she wanted no intimacy with him." How much intimacy do you want with the King?

   _____

   _____

2. "God's bride will have attributes of Queen Esther; she will come when the King calls and she will dress in the apparel that He chooses for her." Do you respond to the King when he calls?

   _____

   _____

3. "Are we willing to stay where God has placed us to help equip the bride and protect her, for such a time as this?" What do you do when you're tempted to run from where God has placed you?

   _____

   _____

## Chapter Thirteen

# Who is this Mysterious Woman Named Mary?

*And behold, a woman in the city who was a sinner, when she knew that Jesus sat at the table in the Pharisee's house, brought an alabaster flask of fragrant oil, and stood at His feet behind Him weeping; and she began to wash His feet with her tears, and wiped them with the hair of her head; and she kissed His feet and anointed them with the fragrant oil.*

LUKE 7:37-38 NKJV

There is much controversy surrounding the Marys of the Bible. I decided I would go beyond all that and just talk about how they loved Jesus, and were willing to take their love and friendship with Him, even to His death.

There were many women named Mary in Jesus' day, and I'm not exactly sure who is who as Scripture doesn't always make it clear. It really doesn't matter; I'm not trying to build a doctrine. I want to go deeper than doctrine and look at the expressions of love that they showed for Jesus.

One day, a Pharisee asked Jesus to come eat with him and Jesus accepted the invitation. I'm sure it was not because he liked Jesus; it was probably because he was trying to get something on Him so he could accuse Him before the council. Right in the middle of their meal, a woman, a sinner, walks in without an invitation, having with her an alabaster flask of fragrant oil. I can only imagine what that Pharisee must have felt when this woman boldly walked into his house. I wonder if he might have been one of her gentleman friends. After all, she was a sinner and it seems as though she knew her way around the house pretty well. Where did she get that oil that typically only the wealthy would have had? Could it have been that the Pharisee gave it to her as a gift? We don't know for sure, so we won't accuse him. Just a thought!

Now let's look at the expression of love she showed for Jesus. As soon as she walked in, she began to cry, dropped to her knees, and started kissing His feet. The tears that fell were so many that they actually washed the sand off Jesus' feet. This sinful woman then let her hair down and began wiping His feet with it. She broke open the alabaster flask and anointed His feet as she kissed them.

This woman had a revelation of the death of Jesus even before His disciples did. As I said, maybe she had been prospering from her sin and that is why she poured the oil out on Him. Maybe that was her way of saying, "I will no longer prosper from my sin, I give it all to You." She obviously had a revelation that He was the Messiah. She saw Him take her sin upon Himself and she was forever thankful that she would no longer have to live in bondage. She truly became His friend.

As the Pharisee watched all this going on, he declared, "If this man were really a prophet, he would know who and what manner of woman this is that is touching him" (Luke 7:39 *paraphrased*). Of course I then ask myself, "How did he know that she was a 'bad girl?'" It doesn't matter. What matters is that in that moment, she loved Jesus with all her heart and gave Him all she had.

When we pour our sin out on Jesus, it releases a beautiful fragrance. When the woman did this, it gave Jesus an opportunity to minister to the Pharisee. He reminded him that when He had entered his house, the Pharisee did not even offer to wash his feet; but when this sinner came in she never stopped kissing His feet. The Pharisee didn't think that Jesus had anything he needed.

> ***When we pour our sin out on Jesus, it releases a beautiful fragrance.***

> *"Therefore I say to you, her sins, which are many, are forgiven, for she loved much. But to whom little is forgiven, the same loves little." Then He said to her, "Your sins are forgiven."*
> LUKE 7:47-48 NKJV

We don't know for sure who this woman was, but one thing we can be sure of is that she loved Jesus and became His friend. And I am almost sure that she was one of the women at the tomb on that dreadful day. I would even go so far as to say that she probably helped prepare the spices for His burial.

After Jesus left the Pharisee's house, He went through every city and village, preaching and bringing the glad tidings of the Kingdom of God. The twelve disciples were with him, and there were also women with him, Mary Magdalene, out of whom had come seven demons, Joanna,

Susanna, and many others who provided for Him from their substance (Luke 8:1-3 *paraphrased*). These women were friends of the Bridegroom before they ever knew He was the Bridegroom. Jesus had many friends who supported His ministry; some were friends who didn't realize who He was until after His death.

Mary of Bethany was also a faithful friend of Jesus. She loved Him with all her heart and worshiped at His feet whenever He came to her house. Martha, her sister, loved Jesus but she did not have the intimacy with Jesus that Mary had. This is the difference between having a ministry to people rather than a ministry to Him. I have watched as God has called many away from ministering to people, to a place within Himself. Some have big platforms and a lot of recognition, which makes it very hard to draw away with only Him. They feel that they have reached their destiny, but sometimes God has a much higher calling in certain seasons of our lives. We must always have our ear open to Him and not just to people.

Jesus loved to go to the house of Mary, Martha and Lazarus because they ministered to Him. It was not just another religious place to visit, it was a place where He could worship His Father as well as be worshiped by them. Of course we see the different levels they were on with their worship. Martha was busy, busy, busy, but she was meeting the physical needs of her guest; Lazarus waited to be called to sit at the table with Jesus. All these things are necessary, but God's very best is found where we find Mary, sitting at Jesus' feet.

Mary loved spending time with Jesus more than the physical things of life. As a result of spending so much time with Him, she was able to get a deeper revelation of the beloved Bridegroom before He had even gone to the Cross.

It was on the sixth day before Passover and Jesus came to Bethany, to the house of Mary, Martha and Lazarus. As Martha worked very hard in preparing a meal for the lot of them, I believe Mary was pondering what she could do for Jesus. But as Mary pondered, her heart was overwhelmed with the love that she was feeling for Him. Without another thought she gets up and goes into her bedroom where she has been keeping a very expensive flask of oil for such a time as this. She has been saving it for over a year now. As she entered the room where Jesus was sitting, her heart must have been pounding with wonder. Would He misunderstand her motive? Would it be appropriate for her, a woman, to touch the feet of a man? Finally, Mary just dropped down on her knees in front of Jesus and began to cry as she broke open the flask of oil to anoint His feet. As she poured the oil over Jesus' feet, the whole room was filled with the fragrance. What else was there to do but worship Him just as she always had? But now Mary didn't have to explain why she loved to sit at the feet of Jesus; it was very obvious to everyone.

Of course there are always those who call themselves friends of Jesus, but when the test comes their hearts reveal their true motives. Look at Judas Iscariot. Before the glory filled the room, you could not have distinguished him from any of the other disciples. When the true anointing is in the house, it reveals who Jesus' friends really are.

> *But one of His disciples, Judas Iscariot, Simon's son, who would betray Him, said, "Why was this fragrant oil not sold for three hundred denarii and given to the poor?" This he said, not that he cared for the poor, but because he was a thief, and had the money box; and he used to take what was put in it.*
>
> John 12:4-6 NKJV

Judas was deceitful and greedy. He could not have cared less about the poor. The Holy Spirit revealed his greed just as He did when Jesus asked the rich young ruler to sell all that he had and give it to the poor. The rich man walked away sorrowfully because he was not willing to give all he had to Jesus. What Jesus was really saying to him was, "Are you willing to do whatever I ask you?" Remember Abraham? He was willing to even give God his own son if that is what He wanted. But God just wanted to see if he was willing. Anyone can say they are His friend, but when the spotlight hits us, it will tell our true story. No one ever knows who their real friends are until the friendship is tested.

> *No one ever knows who their real friends are until the friendship is tested.*

What about the day they crucified Jesus? Who were His friends then? There were lots of folks who had been healed by His hands; many had had demons cast out of them, and many of their children had been set free. But on that day, the ones whom He'd healed, set free, and raised from the dead were in the crowd that mocked Him. They were the ones who cried out, *"Let Him be crucified!"* They even said they were willing to put His blood upon their children (Matthew 27:23;25 *paraphrased*). How crazy is that? After His death, His friend Joseph of Arimathea was willing to care for Jesus' body, wrap Him in clean linen, and give Him his tomb for burial.

> *When Joseph had taken the body, he wrapped it in a clean linen cloth, and laid it in his new tomb which he had hewn out of the rock; and he rolled a large stone against the door of the tomb, and departed.*
>
> MATT. 27:59-60 NKJV

If we are His friends, we will be willing to go all the way to the Cross with Him and then to the tomb where He resurrected. We will be willing to take care of the Body of Christ.

> *Then the disciples went away again to their own homes. But Mary stood outside by the tomb weeping, and as she wept she stooped down and looked into the tomb.*
>
> JOHN 20:10-11 NKJV

Mary Magdalene was a true friend of Jesus. She never gave up; she was with Him all the way. Her first visit to the tomb was very early in the morning while it was still dark. It was not only dark outside, it was also a very dark time for Mary and the disciples. They had lost the One whom they had loved and trusted with all of their hearts. The words that He had once spoken to them were now also clothed in the darkness. Their faith was shattered and now they didn't even know where His body was. I remember when I walked through the dark night of my soul and I could not find the Body of Christ to cling to. My church was gone, and the ones I thought were friends to me and Jesus, had joined in with the mob to kill us.

How many times I have been in Mary's place, crying out, "Where is my Lord?" I relate to Mary as she was so distraught when she thought she had lost her best friend, Jesus. Overwhelmed with grief, all she could do was stoop down and look into the tomb and cry. Then like many of us, she saw Jesus in the garden and didn't know Him. When God takes us into seasons where we've never walked before, it can be hard to recognize Jesus. Oh, but when He calls us by our names as He did Mary, our hearts melt within us, and we cry out *"My Lord and my God!"* (John 20:28 NKJV). Then, because of the awesome experience we have had with Him, we are able to tell others where He is.

We all go through seasons of not knowing where He is, losing our vision, and His words fading away. Maybe we have heard His word that says we will reach the nations for Him, only to find that we never leave our own hometown. Maybe we've read that we will do even greater things than He did, like healing the sick, only to see someone dying after we've prayed for them all night. We know deliverance has been promised to us, but we still see our families bound with drugs and alcohol and demons. We hear Him call to us to come out of the boat and walk on the water, only to see ourselves sinking down beneath the waves of doubt.

These are the times when we must love and trust Him enough to stay with Him as Mary did. Sometimes we need to sit at the tomb where we think nothing is happening, and just wait. If we are His friends, we will go far enough with Him that we won't want to run back to what we were familiar with before we met Him. The words that He has spoken will surely come to pass. We must believe and trust that He sees everything we go through and He *will* come again. Jesus wants us to believe by faith. That means even when we don't see Him.

> *Jesus said to him, "Thomas, because you have seen Me, you have believed. Blessed are those who have not seen and yet have believed."*
>
> JOHN 20:29 NKJV

Another friend of Jesus was His mother, Mary. Out of all His friends, she was the very best. That's why I've saved her till last. Imagine a young girl about thirteen years old betrothed to a wonderful man like Joseph. They would not be married for some time, but when a girl was betrothed to a man, it was the same as being married. In those days the laws forbade a girl to look upon another man other than her dad or brothers, after she had been betrothed.

I bet there were many girls at that time thinking that they might be the one who would fulfill the prophecy of the blessed Savior. But there was only one who found favor with God. What would ever cause this young girl to be the one to birth Jesus, the Son of God? What did God see in her that caused Him to choose her? I believe God saw the same thing in her that He is looking for today. Those who are called by God the Father are called to holiness and purity as the women were in Mary's day.

I know some say that everything is predestined by God. They believe if God has called them to do a mighty work on the earth, it will just happen, there is nothing they have to do. I personally don't believe that for one minute. Mary had the same opportunity to be a prostitute as any of the other girls did, just as women do today. We all have a choice to do good or evil. What were some of the qualities in Mary that were needed in a girl who was called to birth the Son of God?

- She had to be betrothed to the right man
- She had to be a virgin
- She was highly favored of God
- She walked with God and He was with her
- She had faith to believe the impossible
- She was a humble servant
- She had a desire to be with others with the same faith

When the angel came to Mary she could have just as well have said, "no way!" But she yielded herself to God and said, *"Behold the maidservant of the Lord! Let it be to me according to your word"* (Luke 1:38 NKJV). There were many things that Mary would have facing her if she accepted the desire of God's heart to birth His Son. She had to be willing to give up Joseph, her love, if he could not accept that she was pregnant with the Messiah. She knew by the law that she could be stoned to death. But she was willing to stand in shame, knowing that God would protect her. Willing to separate herself from the crowd, she went to the house of Elizabeth and Zacharias. They too were expecting, Elizabeth was pregnant and about to birth the impossible. When we are carrying a call from God in our wombs, we need to separate ourselves from the crowd and find the ones who are pregnant with the same thing.

There were lots of other girls in the city, but Mary was set apart from them. What if Mary had chosen to hang with them all day? I'm sure they laughed at and mocked her, maybe even called her a loose woman. Instead Mary chose to go where she would hear the words of Elizabeth—words that would bless her.

> *And it happened, when Elizabeth heard the greeting of Mary, that the babe leaped in her womb; and Elizabeth was filled with the Holy Spirit. Then she spoke out with a loud voice and said, "Blessed are you among women, and blessed is the fruit of your womb!"*
>
> LUKE 1:41-42 NKJV

Mary had a lot of responsibility weighing on her. She would have to raise the Son of God and still be human. As Jesus grew, Mary would have to spend more time with God in order to hear Him, so she would know how to take care of the Messiah. We may be tempted to think that Mary was different from us, but she wasn't. She was carrying the Body of Christ inside her womb, just as we are carrying Him in our hearts. If we are friends of the Bridegroom, we too have an awesome responsibility to the Body of Christ.

I want to also mention Joseph, Mary's husband. He was another great friend of God, although not talked about much. How many other men would be willing to walk with their wife after hearing her say, "God visited me and said that I am pregnant with His Son?" It may sound crazy, but there have been women who have died short of fulfilling the call that God put within their wombs (hearts) because their husbands would not seek God's face to hear Him say, *"Fear not…for that which is conceived in her is of the Holy Spirit"* (Matthew 1:20 KJV).

Isn't it something that this man named Joseph loaned Mary's womb to Jesus until it was time for His birth, and Joseph of Arimathea loaned his tomb to Jesus until the time of His resurrection? These men called Joseph were definitely friends of God.

The reason I say that Joseph loaned Mary's womb to Jesus is that he knew in his heart that he was not to have an intimate relationship with her until after the Messiah was born. I can't even begin to imagine what Joseph must have felt like the night Jesus was born. He helped Mary deliver our Savior. He actually watched the head of Jesus crowning and was the very first one to lay eyes on Him, even before Mary! How awesome that must have been!

If we are friends of God, He will allow us to see things of the Kingdom before the world even knows they're being birthed. We are living in the end time and once again, Jesus is about to come into the world. Who will be His friends? Who will be waiting at the opening of heaven, anticipating the crowning of His head?

> *If we are friends of God, He will allow us to see things of the Kingdom before the world even knows they're being birthed.*

> *And I heard, as it were, the voice of a great multitude, as the sound of many waters and as the sound of mighty thunderings, saying, "Alleluia! For the Lord God Omnipotent reigns! Let us be glad and rejoice and give Him glory, for the marriage of the Lamb has come, and His wife has made herself ready."*
>
> REVELATION 19:6-7 NKJV

We, as friends of Bridegroom, must live crucified lives. All that is in us that is not yet renewed, must die. God is not looking for someone who is only concerned for themselves, but those who will lay their lives down for Him so His bride can be brought to complete maturity. There is a secret place that God has for those who are willing to climb the stairway to be transformed from glory to glory. The King is looking for those whom He can share His plans and heart with, and the only way that can happen is if we ascend upward with the risen Christ. One who is only wishing to gain something for himself or herself would not think it a serious thing to sin, but the servant of the Bridegroom is not willing to excuse even the smallest sin.

## Questions for Reflection

1. "Martha, her sister, loved Jesus but she did not have the intimacy with Jesus that Mary had." Are you more comfortable serving Jesus or having intimacy with Him?

   _____

   _____

2. "Jesus wants us to believe by faith. That means even when we don't see Him." Do you believe, even when you don't see?

   _____

   _____

3. "The servant of the Bridegroom is not willing to excuse even the smallest sin." How do you think about sin? Is it a serious thing to you?

   _____

   _____

## Chapter Fourteen

# The Bride Has Made Herself Ready

*"Let us be glad and rejoice and give Him glory, for the marriage of the Lamb has come, and His wife has made herself ready."*

REVELATION 19:7 NKJV

There is nothing more beautiful than the Song of Solomon which gives expression of His love, and causes us to feel the intimacy between the bride and Groom. Song of Solomon is an allegory written so well that you can smell the spices and pleasant fruits of His garden that He has prepared for His Bride.

*Your plants are an orchard of pomegranates With pleasant fruits, Fragrant henna with spikenard, Spikenard and saffron, Calamus and cinnamon, With all trees of frankincense, Myrrh and aloes, With all the chief spices—A fountain of gardens, A well of living waters, And streams from Lebanon.*

SONG OF SOLOMON 4:13-14

As the story opens, we see the Shulamite maiden is lovesick. Like all young maidens, she is thinking about her prince in shining armor, coming to rescue her from all her mother's discipline and all her brothers' abuse. Not only is she tired of the abuse, she's tired of working in her mother's vineyards until her skin was cracked and sunburned. How could the love of her life ever think her to be beautiful, her face so black from being in the sun all day and her body scarred from the beatings she'd endured?

> *Thinking she is alone and that no one will hear, she begins to sing a love song to the lover of her soul: "Let him kiss me with the kisses of his mouth—For your love is better than wine. Because of the fragrance of your good ointments, Your name is ointment poured forth; Therefore the virgins love you. Draw me away!"*
> 
> SONG OF SOLOMON 1:2-4 NKJV

Initially, we see the maiden as very young and immature, but she is on her way to maturity. The Shulamite maiden represents the Church growing from glory to glory. There must be a love cry coming from those who crave true intimacy with Jesus. The maiden becomes dissatisfied with working in the flesh; she wants a deeper relationship with the one she had seen standing behind the lattice, calling her to rise up and come away with Him. Of course, she really never dreams that He loves her enough to come and knock on her door and wake her in the middle of the night: *"Rise up, my love, my fair one and come away"* (Song of Solomon 2:10 NKJV).

One night when she least expects it, she hears a knock on her door. To get up and answer would mean that she would have to get dressed, and not only that, she would later have to wash her feet again to return to bed. She has just taken off her robe and gotten comfortable; how could she make such a sacrifice? I wonder how many times Jesus has come to our door and knocked, simply because we have called out to Him and told Him how much we love him, and want to be with Him, only to find ourselves making excuses why we can't come to the door at that time.

> *I have taken off my robe; how can I put it on again? I have washed my feet; How can I defile them?*
> SONG OF SOLOMON 5:3 NKJV

Once the maiden realizes that it was her beloved, she rises up to open the door only to find him gone; she has hesitated too long. *"I opened for my beloved, but my beloved had turned away and was gone"* (Song of Solomon 5:6 NKJV). So many times we have hesitated too long, and when we decide to open the door to Him, He is gone. We are blessed and our hearts leap within us when we smell the fragrance He has left, but now we must run after Him and find Him in another place.

You see, Jesus is not hiding from us because He is punishing us; He is hiding Himself so we will run after Him. *"My beloved is like a gazelle or a young stag. Behold he stands behind our wall; He is looking through the windows, Gazing through the lattice"* (Song of Solomon 2:9 NKJV).

> ***Jesus is hiding Himself so we will run after Him.***

> *"Behold, I stand at the door and knock. If anyone hears My voice and opens the door, I will come in to him and dine with him, and he with Me.*
> REVELATION 3:20 NKJV

As the maiden becomes more mature, she realizes that she must leave her place of comfort and go to the highlands.

> *The voice of my beloved! Behold, he comes Leaping upon the mountains, skipping upon the hills. My beloved spoke, and said to me: "Rise up, my fair one and come away. For lo, the winter is past. The flowers appear on the earth; The time of singing has come, And the voice of the turtledove is heard in our land. The fig tree puts forth her green figs. And the vines with the tender grapes give a good smell. Rise up, my love, my fair one, and come away!*
>
> SONG OF SOLOMON 2:8;10-13 NKJV

Until now, the maiden has been very satisfied with the level she has been on with her beloved, but her capacity has grown and she is now ready to go to a much higher place. Mountains in the Bible symbolize kingdoms; therefore, he is taking her to live in a kingdom realm. She is now getting a greater revelation of who he really is. She now sees him leaping over mountains, so this assures her that she can trust him to take her with him to the high places.

The Church, the Bride of Christ, is receiving a deeper revelation of the greatness of God and the power of His resurrection. God is revealing His Kingdom to His bride where she will also leap over mountains in great victory over the powers of darkness of this world. She will one day stand with Him and rule all nations. The Church will reign and rule over every mountain of the earth.

> *But hold fast what you have till I come. And he who overcomes, and keeps My works until the end, to him I will give power over the nations—"He shall rule them with a rod of iron; They shall be dashed to pieces like the potter's vessels."*
>
> REVELATION 2:25-27 NKJV

The maiden is now walking in the in the power of his love. She is mature enough that He can speak words of affirmation to her without fear of losing her to the spirit of pride. It is the season now for God to speak open revelation to His bride; she is ready to hear the deeper things from His heart. She has grown through the season where she could not bear the depth of His intimacy (see John 16:12).

> *O my love, you are as beautiful as Tirzah, Lovely as Jerusalem, Awesome as an army with banners!*
> Song of Solomon 6:4 NKJV

Song of Solomon expresses the love and intimacy between a bride and her groom like no other book. As we can see from the beginning to the end of the story, the Shulamite maiden is pressing forward to enter into a rest with her beloved. She started out with desiring her own will, but as she ran after him she fell more and more in love with him. There were times when she just wanted to lay down and not get up again, but then she would hear his voice or see his hand and it would cause her once again to rise up from her sleep and continue on her journey.

As we come to the end of this great love story, we find the maiden coming out of the wilderness leaning upon her beloved. She has come into the resting place that he has prepared for her. She no longer doubts his love, she has grown into maturity, and now she knows that he has always been with her even when she walked in dark places. The maiden can now say, *"Set me as a seal upon your heart"* (Song of Solomon 8:6 NKJV). She has totally committed her life to him and has entered into rest.

> *I am a wall, And my breast like towers; Then I became in his eyes as one who found peace.*
> Song of Solomon 8:10 NKJV

She has realized these truths:

- I am a wall … I am mature.
- My breast are like towers … I am balanced and ready to feed others.
- I became in his eyes as one who found peace … I have received revelation of who he truly is, and he sees himself in my eyes.

Like the Shulamite, the Church is at the end of her journey. She is entering into His rest (the Sabbath) where she will no longer struggle with the flesh or walk in her soul realm. The Church is coming out of the wilderness leaning upon her Beloved. Jesus was led up by the Spirit into the wilderness to be tempted by the devil, but He triumphed over evil. This was a revelation of the Church coming out of the wilderness with great victory, because Jesus already did it. Jesus said to him, *"Away with you, satan! For it is written, 'You shall worship the Lord your God, and Him only you shall serve'"* (Matthew 4:10 NKJV). Everything that Jesus did was a revelation for the Church to interpret.

> *For he who has entered His rest has himself also ceased from his works as God did from His.*
> HEBREWS 4:10 NKJV

Remember, the Church is the winner! She will come out with victory, and she will sit upon the throne with the Bridegroom. The friends of the Bridegroom will become one with the bride, and all will sing together a new song, *"Alleluia! Salvation and glory and honor and power belong to the Lord our God!"* (Revelation 19:1 NKJV).

> *And the Spirit and the bride say, "Come!" And let him who hears say, "Come!" And let him who thirsts come. Whoever desires, let him take the water of life freely.*
> REVELATION 22:17 NKJV

## Questions for Reflection

1. "How could the love of her life ever think her to be beautiful?" How does it make you feel to hear that Jesus calls you beautiful? Do you believe this?

   _____

   _____

2. "We must run after Him and find Him in another place." When you can't find Jesus, what do you do?

   _____

   _____

3. "She has grown through the season where she could not bear the depth of His intimacy." Can you bear the intimacy of God, or do you run from it?

   _____

   _____

*The friends of the Bridegroom will become one with the bride!*

www.ingramcontent.com/pod-product-compliance
Lightning Source LLC
LaVergne TN
LVHW052254070426
835507LV00035B/2890